THE STUDY OF LOCAL POLITICS

STUDIES IN POLITICAL SCIENCE

The Study of Local Politics

A MANUAL

by

William H. Riker

University of Rochester

Foreword by Rhoten A. Smith

Citizenship Clearing House

Random House
New York

Sixth Printing, May 1967

Library of Congress Catalog Card Number: 59-6787

Manufactured in the United States of America

FOREWORD

For some years now the Citizenship Clearing House, through its national office and its state and regional affiliates, has been engaged in the development of a broad-gauged program aimed at the improvement of political education in the United States. One of the most important aspects of this program has been the stimulation and encouragement of the use of field research in politics as a teaching device.

Several years of experimentation and experience with the utilization of undergraduate students in field work and field research in politics have clearly demonstrated two basic facts. In the first place, undergraduates, properly guided and supervised, can successfully participate in empirical research inquiry of considerable sophistication. And second, such participation *works*—as a pedagogical device complementing (but not supplanting) the more traditional teaching methods in political science, and as a stimulant to a heightened interest on the part of the student in personal participation in the political process.

Both of these aims lie very close to the central concern of the Citizenship Clearing House. A student is motivated toward an active concern for politics, if at all, only through a deepened and more meaningful understanding of the political process and the crucial role it plays in a democracy, and through an actual and personal, rather than vicarious, involvement in political affairs. Thus, the hundreds of political scientists who are active in the program of CCH are convinced that the use of laboratory methods is fully as important in the teaching of political science as it is in the teaching of physics or chemistry.

There has long been a need for a manual of field research in political science, prepared especially for the undergraduate student who may have virtually no background in research methods and who is often dismayed when faced with the imposing terminology used in more technical and advanced works. Professor Riker has met this pressing need in the present volume. In simple and direct language he introduces the student to the subject of field research in politics, showing how to develop a project, what to look for, and whom to talk to, and providing a wealth of valuable suggestions and insights on research techniques. At the same time, through the bibliography and appendices, the groundwork is laid for more advanced field research for those students who continue in political science.

As one who has used field research projects for undergraduates in his own teaching for a number of years, I cannot refrain from adding one observation in support of such projects as a method of instruction. It is this: though an increased understanding of the American political process on the part of the students is its greatest justification, one cannot overlook the fact that the instructor can learn much himself from the research of his students. American politics is not only a vast field, it is an ever-changing one, and those who teach the subject need the help and insight, not only of their colleagues but of their students as well, to complement their own research and study.

Rhoten A. Smith, Director
Citizenship Clearing House
New York, New York

CONTENTS

THE STUDY OF LOCAL POLITICS

CHAPTER I

Field Research in Political Science and the Study of Local Politics

Although political science is often thought of as a library-bounded discipline, it is actually deeply dependent on field research, as much so indeed as is anthropology. The business of political science is to formulate hypotheses about a particular kind of human behavior, that is, political behavior, and, once the hypotheses are formulated, to test them by whatever techniques are available. The only way I know to carry on either activity is to observe political behavior. Ultimately, this involves some sort of field research—talking to politicians, measuring the way people behave politically, etc. Hypotheses or tentative generalizations are formulated out of a consciousness of many discrete observations and they are tested by determining how well they fit other behavior observed by the tester. This does not mean there is no role in political science for the use of statistical techniques or for the interpretation of documents (which are themselves a record of behavior); it merely means that this work too is basically dependent on hypotheses from observation and is ultimately verified in terms of observation.

Since the observation of political behavior is a key element in the discipline, the technique of field work is one of the things that every undergraduate student of government should learn, along with political theory and various verified generalizations that have resulted from other persons' observation. Since there is no volume that provides instruction in the arts of field technique, this Study is intended to fill this gap, at least partially, by providing a manual of field methods for the study of one kind of political behavior, what we call, for lack of a better name, local politics.

Field research on the subject of local politics is particularly attractive for undergraduates for a number of reasons. Naturally, fledgling political scientists cannot talk to Presidents or Congressmen, or at least not for long enough to learn much; but they can talk to assemblymen, councilmen, some mayors, local party chairmen, precinct captains, and the like. These latter people, who are the ones who know about local politics, are relatively accessible to students, especially when the students are prospective constituents. As many teachers of political science have discovered in the last decade or so, local politicians are willing to spend an incredible amount of time talking to college students. Hence, one major advantage of studying political behavior as it appears on the local scene is that the actual participants are available to students for interviewing and observation.

A second reason why the study of local politics is particularly attractive for undergraduates is that the heart of American politics is local politics. By way of contrast, in England or France, for example, political parties are centralized organizations run by national leaders who are often able to control the nominations of candidates for local office. But our politics is not like that. The national party organization is rudimentary; the national party leaders, such as the President or the Presidential candidate, have little or nothing to say about the personnel or ideology of the local party groups; and indeed the local politicians are often able to defy national leaders on major party programs or policy. In fact, one may say that the national leaders, far from being able to chose local leaders, are in fact themselves chosen by local leaders, while the local leadership groups are self-perpetuating. Not surprisingly, therefore, much of our national policy is the product of compromise among the ambassadors of local political organizations, ambassadors who sit in the House and Senate and the national party conventions. Hence, if one wishes to understand American politics on the national level, one must first understand local politics in all the variety of traditions, of organizations, of political techniques, and of types of personnel.

A third reason why the study of local politics is particularly attractive for undergraduates is that there is relatively little printed material about it. Hence students must use field methods if they are to learn anything at all. It is true, of course, that political scientists and sociologists and journalists have written some detailed works on local politics. I have constructed in Appendix I a selected bibliography of what seem to me the most useful of these books and essays produced in the last twenty years. What strikes one most forcefully about this bibliography is its brevity. A similar selected bibliography about national politics in the same period would, I am certain, turn out to be at least ten times as long. Both scholars and journalists have, I suppose, tended to regard local politics as ephemeral and have not, therefore, been willing to devote their energies to describing and interpreting it. As a consequence, most of the writing about local politics is relegated to ephemeral sources—newspapers. And often—except in large cities with competing newspapers that have a tradition of complete coverage of local politics—newspaper reporting on local politics is fragmentary and inadequate. Newspapers might indeed be expected to print occasional reviews of the local political situations, but in fact they hardly ever do, probably because they are so deeply engaged in day-to-day reporting that they cannot find either space or energy for feature articles. Occasionally local pressure groups such as chambers of commerce, unions, leagues of women voters, etc. publish pamphlets on local politics. Usually, however, these are much more concerned with municipal administration than with municipal politics. Furthermore, what they do have to say about politics is often heavily slanted in favor of the publisher's interest; and often also the reporting of facts is simply inaccurate. In short, although Americans talk and read much about politics, perhaps more than about any other single subject besides the weather, few detailed and accurate analyses of local politics are available. And what few there are soon come to be out of date. The only adequate sources of information are people—politicians (both professional and amateur), editors and reporters, public officials, etc. In order to question and observe these people, students must use field methods and that is what this manual is intended to help them do.

But not only can a student expect to learn field techniques from this kind of study of local politics; they can also expect certain other, perhaps incidental, but nevertheless valuable results. For one thing, they will perhaps acquire a sense of the structure of politics generally. When one actually sees the formation of a coalition or hears about it from the lips of the political entrepreneur who formed it, one obtains a vivid sense of the bargaining, strategy-planning, leading, etc. that is the heart of politics. It is one thing to read about the strategy and bargaining in history textbooks. It is another to feel a vicarious participation in it only once removed. The latter is in a sense far closer to reality. Then, too, textbooks about politics make many generalizations that constitute in sum the broad interpretation of American politics. But generalizations, like words, are often incomprehensible without knowledge of the events and situations to which they refer. For example, it is often—and quite truly—asserted in theoretical writings that in many neighborhoods in which it is conventionally believed that a two-party system exists, the minority party is only a shadow organization, run by a few fanatics or patronage-hunters, without contact with the voters, politically meaningless and ideologically insignificant. One can comprehend this simple generalization even without practical political experience. But its meaning is more profound and personal after one has tried to find the precinct captain of the minority party and has discovered that he does not exist or after one has attended a caucus of the minority party and actually observed the three old gentlemen and one old lady, all of whom might more profitably have spent the evening watching television. Acquaintance with a few politicians and investigation of a few political events will not, of course, lead to a general understanding of American politics. Even a man who immerses himself for his whole adult life in practical politics will not acquire a general understanding unless he reflects theoretically about his experience. But acquaintance and observation do clarify generalizations. An analogy with natural science is suggestive: One may spend a lifetime as a laboratory assistant and never understand zoology; but it is difficult to be a zoologist without some dissection, experimentation, and field observation.

Another incidental but nonetheless valuable result from the field study of local politics is that students will banish forever from their thinking our cultural stereotype of the politician—fat and paunchy, cigar-chewing, derby-hatted. When this caricature speaks, it is of paving contracts for his friends or street cleaning jobs for his constituents. Sometimes sinister, always banal, he is described by the words Alice Roosevelt Longworth (herself under the influence of the stereotype) is said to have uttered of Warren G. Harding: "He was not a bad man; he was just a slob." This picture of the American politician may once have been true, although I suspect it was invented by "goo-goos"—as professional politicians styled reformers at the turn of the century—as an incident in their struggle for votes. But whether or not the picture was ever true, it is not today. Politicians are, for the most part, typical men of their communities, interested in the things that the community as a whole is interested in, with a standard of honesty at least as high as that of the white collar class generally. The cartoonists' stereotype of the politician is as antiquated and inaccurate as his stereotype of the farmer with an Uncle Sam beard and a conversation that consists largely of "by cracky." While one can, with conscious effort, recognize the distortion, it still lingers on in our thinking. Even those who would deny that they are influenced by it utter the word "politician" with a sneer or explain an event with the deprecatory phrase, "Oh, that's just politics." Back of both utterances is the stereotype. The only way to banish it is to replace it with a memory of real people. And that is just exactly what the field study of local politics will do.

CHAPTER II

The Selection of the Subject: Areas for Field Research and Kinds of Analysis

In undertaking the study of local politics, it is necessary that you study the politics of some particular community. But there are many political units in the United States, 155,000, so the Census Bureau says. The first problem students face, therefore, is the selection of one of these to study. Of course, you have no need to choose among this astronomical number. Convenience limits the choice to several. For much student work, your home town or some civil subdivision of it is often the best choice. The advantage here is, of course, that you already know some of its traditions and problems. Considering that most student research must be done in a brief space of time (a semester, or a summer vacation, or a winter or spring vacation), the fact that one already has some knowledge of the community may be the most compelling influence in the choice of a subject. But there are disadvantages, too, to writing about your home community. Besides the fact that it may be inaccessible from your school during the school year, there are procedural limitations too. If your family or some members of it are closely identified with one political group, you may never be able to establish rapport with leaders of an opposing group. In general, politicians may not speak so freely with local persons as with outsiders. On the other hand, local politicians often feel some responsibility for the political education of a local student, even one with connections in an opposing group, and may well be willing to spend more time with a local student than with an outsider. My general impression is that undergraduates have more success in field research when they study their home communities than when they study a place about which they have previously known very little. Whether you study your home community or another one is, however, a matter of much less importance than whether or not you study carefully and thoughtfully. Hence, convenience seems to me the major consideration in the choice of a community to study.

But even when you have selected a community, there are still several political subdivisions to choose among. At the very minimum every neighborhood is part of a state, of a county (or parish), of a Congressional district, of a state senate district, of a state assembly district, of a township or town. If the neighborhood is urban, it is also in a city, in a ward, and in a precinct. In some parts of the West, it may also be in less common subdivisions like a water district. Often also, school districts and judicial districts are separate from the others. All of these political units elect officials; each has its own unique politics. Which of them can you most conveniently and profitably study? The following considerations ought to guide your choice:

1. *The chosen unit ought to be small enough so that you can conveniently interview its politicians.* Manifestly, the larger the subdivision, the more complex its politics and

the more numerous the people who must be consulted in order to comprehend it fully. Considering that students cannot like anthropologists spend several years interviewing, observing, and absorbing traditions, units as large as a state or a great city probably ought not to be chosen. Congressional districts that stretch over several counties are also too large to be studied adequately by students. On the other hand, congressional districts (like those in New York or Chicago) smaller than a city are sometimes convenient and rewarding areas of study. In most circumstances, however, it is best to study a still smaller unit—a ward or a state assembly district in a large city, a village or school district or county in a rural area, the city itself in a small or medium-sized city. Even so small a unit as a precinct can sometimes be studied profitably. If it is a well organized precinct, the committeeman's activities are themselves interesting. If there has recently been a sharp contest for the committeemanship, that contest can provide a fascinating study, especially if it is associated with an intra-party battle in the ward, city, county, or state. This rarely happens, of course, but when it does the precinct alone is a sufficient area for your attention.

2. *The chosen unit ought to be one in which the chief political figures are accessible to students.* In almost all cases you will find that the people you seek to interview are as eager to talk to you as you are to talk to them. Politicians, like most of us, enjoy talking about themselves and their work. But not all of them have the time to do so. The governor of a state is a busy man, all day, every day of the year. So is the mayor of a large city. So is a senator or representative in Congress, although occasionally you may find that representatives are accessible to you. Even if one of these busy men grants an interview, it will in all likelihood be for only fifteen minutes, which is hardly long enough to learn much from him. It is best, therefore, to choose a unit like a state senatorial district, a ward, a small city, etc. in which the leading figures are, though often busy,

more likely to talk to you for a longer time than fifteen minutes.

3. *The chosen unit ought to be one in which politics are lively*. It is hardly feasible to study a unit, a ward for example, in which there is little party organization, in which one party regularly wins almost by unanimity, in which the alderman is re-elected term after term without opposition either in the primary or general election. There are many such voting units in the United States—villages, towns, school districts, wards, precincts, even counties. It is foolish to study the politics of such subdivisions for then, in effect, you study something that does not exist. A warning, however: Not all electoral units that appear to be without politics are as insipid as they seem. The fact that a unit is traditionally attached to one party does not preclude sharp (though often ephemeral) factionalism within it. The fact that a unit seems apolitical in the selection of its own officials does not preclude a lively political life in the selection of officials of the larger units that contain it. Or again, the fact that state law requires nonpartisan elections precludes neither party activity (half-undercover) nor almost-institutionalized personal politics. Indeed, some of the most fascinating and least understood politics in the United States is within one-party areas and under the cover of officially nonpartisan elections.

You must decide, at least provisionally, upon the subject of your inquiry as well as the voting unit. The kind of questions you ask and the kind of persons you interview and the kind of documentary material you gather depend on the subject as well as the unit. Furthermore, the choice of a unit and the choice of a subject are interdependent. If you study a referendum on a school bond issue, for example, then you must write about the school district in which the election occurred.

Many sorts of analyses of local politics have been made; the kind of research one does for one sort of analysis is often unrelated to the kind one does for another sort. So, early in your field activity, you must make some decisions about just what you are doing. In general, the research on local politics may be divided into three main categories, according to types of research techniques: (A) Community studies research; (B) Research on voting habits; (C) research on the history of a particular event. A word about the theoretical relevance and research techniques of each category of study:

A. *A study of the life of a community as a whole* has often been undertaken by research teams. With reference to politics, the main purpose of these so-called community studies is to discover how political decisions are related to other areas of life, how political leadership is related to other kinds of leadership, etc. The great advantage of such studies is, of course, that they give a balanced and whole picture of a community and avoid the distortions that often result from an overemphasis on politics as such. For this reason, every study of local politics ought to be something of a community study as well. Unfortunately, however, the traditional techniques of community studies are such that undergraduates cannot ordinarily make use of them. Frequently, the studies are conducted over a long period of time by persons from several disciplines. With proper instruction, however, it may be possible for students to undertake such work. In this connection, it is desirable to read some of the reports on community studies that are recorded in Appendix I, especially Vidich and Bensman, *Small Town in Mass Society,* Warner and Lunt, *Social Life in a Modern Community,* and Whyte, *Street Corner Society.*

B. *A study of voting habits* is less difficult than a community study but more difficult usually than the study of the history of an event. The advantage of such a study is, of course, that it provides a general interpretation of the politics of a community. Usually it requires fairly extensive statistical analysis and somewhat sophisticated interviewing and hence holds theoretical pitfalls for the unwary student.

But it does provide a fairly comprehensive and satisfying knowledge of local politics. The series of questions one might attempt to answer in an essay on voting habits are:

1. What have been the results in a series of elections in the unit studied and in subdivisions of the unit (wards of a city, townships of a county, etc.)?
2. Is a consistent pattern shown in these results (that is, do particular subdivisions consistently return majorities of about the same proportion for candidates of one party or faction)?
3. Is there a discernible trend toward change of party allegiance in recent elections?
4. If there is a consistent pattern or a discernible trend, how do local politicians explain them?
5. If local politicians believe voting habits are controlled by some particular characteristic of the population (property ownership, union membership, church affiliation, etc.), can those characteristics be measured in the political subdivisions of the community and correlated with voting in the subdivisions? If so, is the correlation such that one can impute a causal relationship between the characteristic and the voting? (See Chapter IX.)
6. Are there any recent elections in which the stresses and strains which make up the particular pattern or trend are concretely revealed in campaign issues? If so, can such elections be described?
7. Are there distinctive nationality, racial, religious, or economic groups in the community? If so, can you determine whether or not they influence elections significantly?

Those who wish to attempt a study of voting habits should read the eleven chapters in V. O. Key's *Southern Politics* (cf. Appendix I-A), which describe the politics of the eleven states of the old Confederacy. That work, which is an outstanding example of scientific analysis of community politics, can serve as a model for your work. Other works of this nature are described in Appendix I.* For this kind of subject you might also consider using public-opinion polling techniques, in which case you should consult your instructor and read such works as Herbert Hyman, *Survey Design and Analysis: Principles, Cases, and Procedures* (Glencoe, Illinois, The Free Press, 1955), Mildred B. Parten, *Survey, Polls and Samples: Practical Procedures* (New York, Harper, 1950), and Leon Fistinger and

* It must be emphasized that you should never attempt to study the traditions and voting habits of an area without first undertaking field investigation. Sometimes rather shy students think that they can do all their work with election returns gathered in a library and statistically analyzed with a calculating machine. One horrible example is offered to warn you against this temptation. A student, wishing to study the trend of Negro voting in a large northern city, statistically compared the results of selected Negro precincts in the 1954 and 1956 elections and discovered to his amazement that upper-class Negroes (as assigned to class by the average assessed valuation of the precinct) were swiftly changing from Republican to Democratic, while lower-class Negroes were slightly reversing the trend. Even a casual acquaintance with the city's politics would have assured him that this was a false conclusion. He now undertook the field investigation which he had been trying to avoid, expecting to find an unnoticed political trend of major importance. What he found instead was that his upper-class precincts had entirely changed from white to Negro in the period between 1954 and 1956. It was a neighborhood of old but expensive apartments whose occupants had been fairly heavily Republican and who were replaced by mostly Democratic though reasonably prosperous Negroes. On the other hand, his lower-class precincts were ones that had long been occupied by Negroes so that their slight tendency to turn Republican was a characteristic expression of the change in northern Negro votes of that biennium. The moral of the story is: Do not try to make statistical studies until you have investigated the community sufficiently to know what kind of statistical studies are appropriate.

Daniel Katz (editors), *Research Methods in the Behavioral Sciences* (New York, Dryden Press, 1953). Above all, however, you ought to make extensive use of the sources of data described in Appendices II and III.

C. *A study of particular political events* depends less on statistical analysis (although such analysis is often necessary) and more on interview material. Hence it requires more field work and less library work than the others and is, in that sense, more rewarding for experience with field techniques. On the other hand, each particular event is unique and the study of one event hardly permits generalization about a community. Insofar as the event is in some way typical of a class of events, one may generalize on the basis of it. Unfortunately, however, few students are in a position to prove or even to assert that the event they have studied is really typical of a larger class of events.

Still, knowledge of a specific event is valuable, even though it may be unique. Some events which might reasonably be described in this connection are:

1. a primary or election campaign for a local public or party office; for example, a primary campaign for the nomination for sheriff, a campaign for the election of a state representative, a campaign for the election of a ward chairman of a party, etc.
2. a campaign in connection with a local referendum, such as a campaign over a school bond issue, the local portion of a campaign over a referendum on a proposed amendment to the state constitution, etc.
3. a local campaign for a state or national office. (This should not be undertaken unless a distinct local campaign occurred, as, for example, when the competing candidates were actively supported by locally organized and locally directed clubs.)
4. a party caucus for the selection of delegates to state or national conventions.

Many campaigns are comprehended in this list, however, and you may find it difficult to choose among them. I suggest, therefore, that you use the following standards in the selection of a campaign to study: First, the campaign ought to have been hotly contested. A lackadaisical campaign will very likely lead to lackadaisical research. Second, the campaign ought to be recent, at least within the last year and preferably within the last few months. Recent campaigns are easier to study because they are clearer in the memory of all the participants. Campaigns and controversies that have just been completed are probably the best of all because the participants have usually not had enough time to rationalize the outcome. Hence you are likely to obtain the primary reactions of your informants, reactions which are likely to be in accord with the actual spirit of the campaign.

Many accounts of campaigns have been written as parts of books on political history. Some of these are mentioned in Appendix I-D. But the most useful models for student work are Donovan, *Congressional Campaign,* and Harder, *Non-Partisan Election* (see Appendix I-D). Excellent descriptions of recent campaigns are also available in Paul T. David, Malcolm Moos, and Ralph M. Goldman, editors, *Presidential Nominating Politics in 1952* (see Appendix I-B).

CHAPTER III

Who Should Be Interviewed

Inasmuch as the purpose of interviewing in field research on politics is to discover facts, one must talk to those people who know them. For the most part, these are the people in politics. Their information is usually partial and often fragmentary; but they do at least know what they themselves have done. And sometimes they are the only ones who know that.

If you study a particular campaign, then the candidates, their campaign managers, and the party chairmen are the obvious persons to interview. If you write about a Congressional campaign, the successful candidate is probably too exalted a figure to give you much of his time. But his campaign manager and the Congressional district chairman of his party are available, and so, of course, are the defeated candidate, his manager, and the party chairman. In most other cases, all the leading figures are probably available for at least brief interviews. If you write about the voting habits of your community, you ought certainly to talk to the chairmen of both parties for they have doubtless considered that problem often, although not necessarily wisely. When, however, you study a one-party community, you must talk to the leaders of factions within the single party.

Party politicians must, of course, be your primary source of information. No other class of persons can speak with as much authority and knowledge about local politics as they. Nevertheless, some other types of people can give you information, subsidiary information, to be sure, but sometimes valuable. For example, newspaper reporters and editors can, in almost every community, be counted upon to know something about politics. The journalist's trade is to know what has happened; in fact, individual reporters sometimes have more extensive knowledge of politics than do individual politicians. For that reason newspapermen can often be very helpful. There are, however, two disadvantages in interviewing them. One is that they are busy people who have less incentive than politicians to spend time talking to students. The other is that journalists sometimes pretend to omniscience, a pretense that is a kind of trade defect: To admit to lacunae in knowledge is to admit to a deficiency in the journalist's skill. In spite of these disadvantages, however, reporters and editors are often knowledgeable men who can help you greatly.

A third class of persons who usually know something about politics is made up of the paid officials of pressure groups—secretaries of chambers of commerce, business agents of local unions, etc. These people often feel the same public obligation that politicians do to talk to students. Hence you stand a good chance of a friendly reception from them. Furthermore, these officials know much about politics. That is one of the things the group pays them to know. Their knowledge is, however, usually limited to the affairs in which they have been directly involved and they are likely to distort the political picture, magnifying the role that their group plays. Yet, for what they know—and often it is considerable—it is sometimes worth while consulting them.

One kind of person is to be avoided: In every community there are people of a highly political turn of mind who cannot or do not take an active part in politics. Perhaps they fear that identification with a party will hurt their social standing or their business. Perhaps they lack the self-confidence necessary for positions of leadership. At any rate, they compensate for their inactivity by collecting political gossip, which they are eager to relate to all who will listen. Since they have neither the personal experience of politicians and group officials nor the professional observation of journalists, their so-called knowledge is usually a mass of misinformation. They play the same role in politics as the tout plays at the race track and they are to be avoided for the same reason.

As a summary of the foregoing advice, I have here set down a list of suggestions about persons to interview. This list is simply to help you select; it does not imply that you ought to interview someone in each of the classes mentioned, for not only is this unnecessary but also your time is doubtless limited. You must, of course, choose persons to interview from it on the basis of your own judgment. If you are initially inclined to distrust your own judgment, perhaps it is best to start with the party chairmen of the ward or city or county, for they are necessarily deeply involved in politics. *If you do not know who the party chairmen are, a phone call to the local newspaper or the county clerk will invariably get you their names and business addresses*. Once you have started talking to people, you are certain to be given additional suggestions about whom to interview. And when you get these local suggestions, you can then disregard the following list:

Political Party Officials:

- precinct committeemen (or chairmen or captains) of the Democratic and Republican parties
- ward chairmen
- town chairmen
- county chairmen
- state assembly district or state senate district chairmen
- Congressional district chairmen
- (Few communities have all these party officials in even one party. Fewer, if any at all, have them all in both parties.)

Public Officials:

- Legislators:
  - aldermen (or councilmen)
  - state representatives
  - state senators
  - county board (or court) members
  - school board members
  - United States representatives
- Executives:
  - mayors (or village presidents)
  - sheriffs
  - city managers—These are presumably nonpolitical officials, but their office is such that they must know much about local politics.
  - town chairmen (or township trustees)
  - city, town, or county clerks (or registrars)—While these are often almost nonpolitical offices, the incumbents are by their duties brought into daily contact with politics. Some of them are good observers and hence good informants.
- Judicial Officials:
  - elected judges
  - prosecutors

Others:

- campaign managers for candidates in recent, hotly-contested local elections

reporters and editors on the local newspapers
partners in public relations firms who have much campaigning business
chairmen of non-party groups supporting particular candidates—For example, Chairman of the Milwaukee County Proxmire for Governor Club. Often such clubs are paper organizations, mere letterheads for fund-raising. When, however, they actually conduct active campaigns, the officers usually know something about local politics.
secretaries of chambers of commerce
secretaries of local manufacturers' associations
secretaries of local trade and businessmen's associations—secretary of a tavern keepers' league, secretary of a realtors' association
business agents and international representatives of local unions
chairmen of trades and labor councils or industrial union councils

The foregoing list is rather long and your reaction may well be that it might be wisest to start with the most important. Unfortunately, however, it is not possible to say which persons are most important, for the situation varies from state to state. In some states the sheriffs run the county politics and are the most important local officials; in other states county judges play this role. In many cities mayors are the chief figures in local politics; but in others the mayors are elected nonpartisanly and try to avoid identification with politics. If no public official is the key man, then a party official may be; but sometimes, as in Kentucky, for example, the Administration man in each county (that is, the governor's patronage and machine representative in the county) may hold no office whatsoever in either the government or the party. In general, one can find out who is most important in a locality only by interviewing politicians who know.

One final remark on the selection of persons to interview: Alexander Heard, who did most of the interviewing for V. O. Key, *Southern Politics,* discovered that:

> The more self-sufficient the individual, the freer he was to talk. . . . the minions of a political machine refused to talk about matters that their boss discussed with freedom. . . . Politicians on the make proved less inclined to get down to essentials than weathered veterans who had won and lost races for twenty years. In fact, the older and more experienced the politician, the more likely he was to speak freely.*

In your research you will discover that these observations are even more appropriate for you than they were for Mr. Heard. You will find, as he did, that the older, more experienced politicians will speak freely. In addition, you will often find that they adopt a somewhat fatherly attitude toward you. If you are interviewing in your home town, they will want to be sure that you understand its traditions. Often they feel a deep sense of duty to guide youth. At the same time, do not rely too heavily on older men. Their observation is likely to be heavily weighted by the opinions and issues that concerned them in their youth. They find it fairly difficult to think in contemporary terms. They are not so likely to be informed about the practical details of recent controversies as they are about the details of controversies of twenty years ago. If you write about the voting habits of the community, you ought certainly to talk to some of the older men as well as some of the younger men. If you write about a particular event, it is important to talk to the major participants regardless of their age.

* Alexander Heard, "Interviewing Southern Politicians," *American Political Science Review,* Vol. 44 (December, 1950), p. 895.

CHAPTER IV

Planning the Questions

One basic rule of all research is that you cannot get answers unless you ask questions. That rule is applicable here. If you visit a politician, explain your assignment, and then, without asking questions, wait patiently for him to tell you all about the politics of his community, there is likely to be an embarrassing silence. Presently the politician, seeking to smooth out the ruffled situation, may launch into a lecture full of local patriotism, from which you will learn nothing. The interview is then thoroughly shattered and you had best leave politely. If, on the other hand, you go to the interview primed with questions, you can usually keep your informant talking, and talking to the point, even for an hour or two.

It is essential, therefore, that you have a set of questions in mind. And it is equally essential that they be good questions, for it is a second basic rule of all research that you cannot expect useful answers to inept or uninformed questions. If you ask an indefinite question like "What are politics like here in Podunk?", you have only yourself to blame if the whole answer is "Pretty quiet." For the most part, your informants will be practical men, not accustomed to theoretical reflection. Alexander Heard, in the essay just quoted, remarked: ". . . efforts to obtain 'interpretation' of political phenomena were disappointing. Few of the practitioners had an appreciation of the social significance of their activities." Consequently, you cannot address theoretical questions to them, questions which your instructor might answer readily (too readily, perhaps). Instead, you must approach your informants with specific questions about their own experiences in practical politics.

One way to find a set of quite specific questions is to compile recent election returns for the community. A study of them is likely to reveal patterns, trends, and anomalies, all of which you can discuss during interviews. These data are most easily obtained from state Blue Books or legislative manuals. The *Wisconsin Blue Book,* for example, contains primary and general election returns by precinct, ward, village, and town for every state and national election in the previous biennium. But not all states publish manuals and not all the manuals have detailed election returns. (Appendix II contains a list of the state manuals that have good election data.) And, of course, none of the state manuals contain returns for local elections. When, for one of these reasons, the state Blue Book or legislative manual is not usable, you can get the returns from your city or county clerk or registrar. (Newspaper files usually have some data; but they are not always accurate, that is, they are often the first returns, reported before the canvassing is complete.)

Some typical questions that are likely to come out of a study of election returns are:

1. Why does one subdivision of the community consistently return majorities for one party (or faction) while the rest of the subdivisions consistently return majorities for the other party (or faction)?
2. Why are the majorities for one official so much larger than the majorities for candidates of the same party for other offices? Why, for example, did the Republican candidate for state treasurer, who ran no better in the state than the ticket as a whole, run far ahead of the ticket, in this community? Was there a special campaign for him locally? If so, what was its nature? Or, for another example, why did the Democratic candidate for President receive a majority of the votes of the community while ordinarily the community votes heavily Republican?
3. Why has the average majority for one party been increasing (or decreasing) in recent years?
4. Are some wards (or precincts or towns) more effectively organized than others by one or both of the parties? If so, does this superior organization have an influence on the number of voters and the majorities obtained?

Often your initial informants can recall a particularly interesting recent campaign. If you interview its main participants, you can ask all the questions just suggested and many more related to the specific election itself. Typical questions which you might ask candidates and their campaign managers are:

Questions on Organization:

(Questions on organization, which require specific and technical answers, start an interview effectively. They are easily answered and hence they accustom the informant to the conversation.)

1. How was your side of the campaign organized? That is, did one person run the whole campaign or were specific jobs given to specific people?

2. If the work was divided, who did what jobs?
3. If you had a committee, was it active? What did it do?
4. What help, if any, did the regular party organization give?
5. How many people were actively engaged in the campaign?
6. What help did pressure groups (trade associations, labor unions, etc.) give you?

Questions on Advertising:

7. What advertising mediums did you use to put your issues and your personality before the public?
   A checklist of mediums:
   - public meetings
   - radio
   - television
   - newspaper advertising
   - newspaper stories
   - billboards
   - yard signs, store window signs, utility pole signs
   - bumper stickers, car window signs, signs for the tops of automobiles
   - sound trucks
   - direct mailing
   - door-to-door canvassing and leaflet distribution
   - lapel buttons, match covers, novelty pencils, etc.
8. Can you give an example of each medium used?
9. If newspaper stories were used, how did you get the stories into the papers?
10. If direct mailing was used, who addressed the cards and envelopes?
11. If door-to-door canvassing was used, who did it?
12. If signs of any sort were distributed, who distributed them and who used them?
13. If public meetings were used, who sponsored the meetings?

14. Did the meetings attract large or small attendance? That is, were they effective means of reaching the public?
15. Did you speak at meetings of clubs, such as luncheon clubs, veterans' organizations, chambers of commerce, labor unions, women's civic clubs, etc.?
16. Which of all the mediums used were, in your opinion, most effective? Why?
    (This question might be asked in this form: If you had the campaign to do over, would you use different mediums of advertising? Would you change the emphasis among them?)

Questions on Money:

(Questions about money are, of course, often delicate ones. They will arise naturally enough in the conversation, however, if they are asked at exactly this point, that is, just after a series of questions about the use of money for advertising.)

17. How much did the campaign cost?
18. How was the money divided among the various advertising mediums?
19. How did you finance the campaign?
20. Who were the chief contributors?

(If your informant asserts that he financed his whole campaign himself, it is appropriate to express some surprise in the hope that he will add, "Well, I got a little money from so-and-so or from such-and-such an organization." That is your cue to inquire about the amount.)

21. Did the political party organization contribute any money?
22. Did any pressure group contribute money?

(If you suspect that your informant may be reticent about the source of his financing, the best order of questions after number 18 is: "Did the party help you out? If so, to what amount?" Then: "Did friends help you out? If so, to what amount? How large were the individual contributions?" Then: "Did organizations help you out? If so, to what amount? How large were the individual contributions?" Placed in this order, the questions do not so easily permit a denial of outside support.)

23. Did you have as much money as you needed? If not, in what ways could you have used more?

Questions on Issues:

24. What issues did you stress?
    Why?
25. Which of your arguments seemed to occasion the most enthusiastic response among:
    a. the adherents of your own party?
    b. marginal voters?
26. If you had it to do over again, would you change your emphasis on particular issues? Would you emphasize different issues?
27. At what time in the campaign did you introduce your chief issue and your chief argument?
28. Why did you choose that time?
29. At what time in the campaign did you make your greatest effort?
30. Do you think that any other timing in the presentation of issues would have made your campaign more successful?
31. Do you think that any other timing in campaigning effort would have made your campaign more successful?

Questions on Support:

32. Were you formally endorsed by any group? (chamber of commerce, labor union, business or trade group, PTA, civic league, etc.)

(If the answer to question 32 is "yes," then you ought of

course to interview an official of the endorsing group in order to ask why the group endorsed him.)

33. Were you informally supported by any group? (church, labor union, business group)
34. Did any of the supporting groups spend money for you (buy newspaper space, buy radio or television time, rent or contribute a hall for meetings, etc.)?
35. Did you have an opportunity to speak to supporting or endorsing groups?

Questions on the Opposition:

36. What do you think was the most effective portion of your opponent's campaign?
37. What was your opponent's strongest issue? (Perhaps: Which one of your opponent's arguments did you spend most time refuting?)
38. What mistakes do you think your opponent made?
39. Do you think that your opponent spent more or less money than you?
40. Do you think that your opponent was fair in his treatment of the issues?
41. Do you think that your opponent was fair to you personally?

Questions on the Outcome:

42. What influences do you give most credit for your success? / failure? That is, do you think it was a question of personality, a question of endorsement (by party or group), a question of campaign techniques, or a question of community traditions?
43. Do you know why this voting unit (ward, town, etc.) voted for / against you?

(Question 43 can be asked of every voting unit. The candidates' answers, if they are well informed, will give you a good survey of the community.)

Questions on the Candidate:

(As indicated in Chapter V, questions about the candidate are sometimes good opening questions.)

44. How long have you been in politics?
45. How did you get your start in politics?
46. What other offices have you held or run for?
47. Why did you decide to run for this office?

(Question 47 is a foolish question to ask a re-elected or defeated incumbent; but it often elicits interesting replies from newly elected incumbents and from defeated candidates who never held the office.)

48. How do you arrange for time off for campaigning and for public service? (if the informant is not self-employed)

Concluding Questions:

49. Who else was deeply involved in your campaign?
50. Do you think it would be worthwhile for me to talk to them?

Two final comments on questions: As you learn more about the particular event and community you are studying, more and more specific questions will occur to you and can be added to this list. Toward the end of your interviewing, specific local questions will probably be greater in number than the list here presented. But do not respect this list too abjectly. Often, instead of questions here suggested, you will find that, once your informant has started talking, you can keep the conversation going much better with simple prompting questions like "Why did you do that?" "What did he say then?" "How did that help you?" etc.

CHAPTER V

How to Begin the Interview

Many students undertake field research reluctantly, fearing that they will be rebuffed by the politicians they seek to interview. Such fear is almost never justified. Indeed, in almost every instance, politicians will welcome you with open arms. Clinical psychologists have long since discovered that most people like to talk about themselves. And while this is characteristic of people generally, politicians have in addition a special and more compelling motive for talking to you. Students are, after all, soon to become voters. And most politicians like to talk to voters, especially to young voters whom they may perhaps in a fatherly way guide into permanent allegiance to the "best" party. It is the politician's business to win votes and you, whatever may be the announced purpose of the visit, are a vote to be won. (This is another reason why it is wisest to study your home town, where you and your parents have a voting residence.) For busy nonpolitical doctors or merchants, a student visit might be simply a nuisance. But for a politician it is *his* opportunity; and *you* should take advantage of it.

In spite of the politician's predisposition to friendliness, misunderstandings and suspicion are always possible. This you wish to avoid. The following paragraphs, therefore, contain a few rules of thumb about starting interviews, rules that, if followed, will probably win you a friendlier reception and allow you to conduct a more successful interview:

1. *Do not worry about proper introductions.* Alexander Heard spent eighteen months interviewing 503 politicians in eleven Southern states. In 39 per cent of the cases he had no introduction at all—not even a name to mention or a letter—to the person whom he interviewed. It was his conclusion that, on the whole, these were his best interviews. He comments:

> When a third person makes the introduction, he thereby usually guarantees the interviewer a courteous reception. In circles skeptical toward outsiders, or among busy people, a proper connection is particularly helpful. Yet, by and large, the ability of the interviewer to create respect for his mission and confidence in his intentions seemed to be more important than the introduction that he brought. In one black-belt town, for instance, the interviewer had impeccable connections. Nevertheless, he had to assure more than one person that he was not a "communist" and had not come as an agent of meddling Yankees. . . .
>
> An introduction by a local partisan sometimes made it hard for the interviewer to convince his informant of his impartiality, for the interviewer seemed to acquire some of the color of his sponsor. When the sponsor and the informant were on the same side of the political fence, this factor might not be a handicap; but it often inhibited the conversation. The presence of third parties obstructed free conversation in somewhat the same way. Informants were invariably restrained in the presence of others, even old cronies.*

* *Ibid.,* pp. 889, 890.

On the basis of this experience, which led to the book *Southern Politics* (already mentioned as a model for your work), you are justified in simply introducing yourself, without seeking the intervention of a third party.

2. *Make your appointment in person.* The chief reason for this advice is that, if the informant sees you long enough to find out what you want, you can usually persuade him to give you at least another fifteen minutes. Furthermore, while a phone call is doubtless more convenient—it might save you a fairly lengthy trip—it is also easier for the prospective informant to turn down a telephoned request. If you call up, you must perforce accept in good faith a plea of insufficient time. If you visit his office or his home, however, and find he is not too busy to see you for at least a moment, then he cannot, without the appearance of insincerity, plead busyness. There are some truly busy persons, however, whom you probably can reach only by phone. It is probably wisest to reserve these prospects in the hope that, after practice in presenting your request in person, it will be smoother and more effective over the telephone.

3. *Start your request for an interview by mentioning your name, your local residence (if appropriate), the place you go to school, and the nature of your project.* The introductory speech might run something like this:

> Good morning, Mr. Doe. I am Richard Roe. I live here in Middletown, out by Garfield Park. I'm a sophomore at Lawrence College. In connection with a course on American government, I am making a study of Middletown politics; and would appreciate it very much if I might talk to you for a little while to get some information. My research is supposed to result in an *objective* and *impartial* description of some aspect of local politics. I have come to see you because I've been told that you know a lot about Middletown politics and I'd be very grateful if you'd talk to me for a little while.

In most instances, this should be enough of an introduction to gain entrance. If, however, the prospective informant displays reluctance, you might add:

> I have found it very difficult to get complete information so that I can make an *objective* study. As I say, many people have suggested that you could help me a lot. I'd like to do a good job on this research project, and so I'd appreciate just a few minutes of your time to ask a few questions.

Such a speech as this is useless, of course, if it is merely parroted. Sincerity in manner and delivery are essential to success. And usually sincerity succeeds. If a sincere appeal to your prospect's pride and pity does not at least start you on an interview, probably nothing will.

If the reluctance seems to be caused only by the pressure of other business, of course, the polite procedure is to offer to come back at another time. When you make such an offer, however, try to arrange for a definite appointment. Thus you might say, "Well, I see you are indeed very busy. Might I come back to see you tomorrow? When would be a convenient time? Perhaps four o'clock in the afternoon?"

In general, your first approach ought to emphasize these three points:

(a) if you are a local person, that this is the case;
(b) that you are a college student;
(c) that you want to do objective and impartial research.

Emphasis on your local origin is intended to awaken your informant's sense of obligation to you as a constituent or prospective constituent. Emphasis on your attendance at college is intended to impress on him the educational nature of the enterprise. Emphasis on "objectivity" and "impartiality" is intended to allay suspicion. Most reluctance, aside from that which grows out of busyness, stems from a distrust of colleges and of academic enterprise generally. Some people on the extreme right regard colleges as hotbeds of radicalism. Some people on the left regard colleges as handmaidens of reaction. As you know, neither picture is correct. But you must recognize the existence of these beliefs and attempt to work around them. Emphasizing the "objectivity" of your proposed research is probably the best way to meet hostility that arises from a political distrust of colleges.

4. *Establish a friendly atmosphere.* There will be few instances of absolute refusal to permit an interview. In eighteen months, only 3 out of 506 Southern politicians refused to talk to Alexander Heard. Of course, he had more time than you and could afford to be more persistent; but on the basis of his experience, it is unlikely that you will be refused even once. What is almost as bad as refusal, however, is an interview in which the informant evades and ignores your questions. You must try, by establishing a friendly atmosphere at the outset of the interview, to overcome the hostility that leads to evasion.

In the great majority of instances, the politician will be as eager to be friendly as you are. These remarks are intended chiefly as advice for those difficult times in which an undertone of hostility disturbs the harmony of the interview.

A number of rhetorical devices can be used to induce friendliness. Most obviously, if you are a member of the same party as the person you are interviewing, do not hesitate to point out that fact when the occasion arises. (On the other hand, it is not only self-defeating but also dishonest to pretend to an affiliation that you do not have.) When you talk to a person of the opposite party, it is, of course, impolitic to parade your opinions. In such circumstances, a discreet silence about party affiliation, an emphasis on your desire for complete and objective coverage, and an expression of your fascination with the political process are rhetorically appropriate attitudes. The ideal situation in such interviews is to leave your informant wondering at the end about your party affiliation. *If a politician of the other party demands point blank what your affiliation is, answer truthfully and straightforwardly and without embarrassment or hesitation—but hasten to add that you want to be open-minded, not only in doing this research but in politics generally.*

Early in the interview, if your informant displays any reluctance at all, stress your dependence on him for information. Point out that no one knows much about local politics except people who are deeply involved in it. Point out also that he is well-known and locally much respected for his activity and that only he can tell you what you need to know. In the American tradition of social relations, such statements are often regarded as flattery, and, for that reason, you may hesitate to utter them. Remember, however, that they are true and that flattery is properly so called only when the statements are false.

One gambit that often helps to create a sympathetic situation at the beginning is to ask the informant for some biographical information. This is especially appropriate when you are interviewing one of the major figures in an event you intend to describe. The first question, then, might run something like this: "Mr. Roe, I have come to you because I would like to write about the recent campaign for alderman. I'd like to ask about your part in it. But first I'd like to know something about you. How long have you been in politics?" And when that is answered, you might ask, "How did you happen to decide to run for alderman?" By the time this latter question is answered, the interview is probably well launched, but further questions of this sort might be: "How did you get into politics in the first place?" and "Just what political work have you done?"

5. *If your informant asks you to keep his comments confidential, promise to do so only if you are willing to preserve his confidence absolutely.* Most interviewers, psychologists, pollsters, etc., begin their interviews with perfunctory assurance that the conversation will be kept confi-

dential. For the purposes of political research, however, such initial assurances seem to be unwise. For one thing, they put the informant on his guard by reminding him that his words may be repeated. For another thing, promises of secrecy are not easily kept. Even professional persons, who ought to have a fine sense of responsibility for their knowledge, repeat facts learned from clients, patients, and students. Commercial public opinion pollsters are possibly the most untrustworthy in this regard. The authors of the Kinsey report, who had special reasons for developing elaborate security precautions, have these comments to make on the careless habits of those who in the regular course of their business promise to keep secrets:

> Few professional people seem to know what it means to preserve the absolute confidence of a record. Professional confidence too often refers to the discussion of individual cases with anyone in the professional fraternity. Such discussions, often in the hearing of secretaries or nurses, soon spread the information abroad, whence it returns to confound the subject who gave his history only after he was guaranteed strict confidence. Professional people connected with the courts too often obtain confessions by promising the confidence of the record, which they promptly betray by carrying the data to court. Academic persons doing research on human case histories regularly turn them over with names attached, to whole classes of students for examination. . . . In penal institutions there are always inmates who are employed in clerical positions, where they have access to the "confidential" records; and information spreads through them to the whole inmate body. . . . Persons who have been betrayed through such sources become, naturally enough, skeptical about contributing further data to any professional person, and it has often been difficult to convince them that our own records would be kept inviolate.*

* Alfred C. Kinsey, Wardell B. Pomeroy, and Clyde E. Martin, *Sexual Behavior in the Human Male* (Philadelphia, W. B. Saunders Co., 1948), p. 46.

Dr. Kinsey and his associates preserved secrecy by means of an elaborate code system, known only to the interviewers, and by carefully refusing to discuss case histories with anyone not professionally connected with the project. Student interviewers are far less capable of preserving confidences. They are not professionally accustomed to keeping secrets: they are not yet sufficiently experienced to regard new and surprising information as simply another fact hardly worthy of repetition; and they do not yet know all the hazards of accidental revelation. Considering these circumstances, it seems better not to promise secrecy.

Many areas of social science are dependent upon informants from the general public. If public trust in the social sciences is broken down by the carelessness of student interviews, then many serious research projects suffer. An analogous situation is found in churches that use the confessional. In all ages they have had to discipline their confessors' tongues in order to maintain confessants' faith in the privacy of confession. They have not always disciplined successfully: and when they have failed they have invariably lost the confidence of their public. For the sake of public trust in the social sciences, therefore, it is best for students to avoid promises that they will find very difficult to keep.

Some of the people you interview may, however, ask for assurances of secrecy. If you give them, you must then be prepared to keep them. You must not discuss the interview with your parents or your friends. You must not talk about it with your college associates, even though they may come from distant places. Geographical mobility is very high in the United States and you cannot be sure where your friends will be a year or two hence. Even if the revelations of the interview seem quite innocuous to you, your judgment gives no license to your tongue, for they may not seem innocuous to your informant or to other people. You must not write them down—either in English or any other language or shorthand read by persons in the United States. In subsequent interviewing you must be careful to phrase questions in such a way that they do not reveal information learned in an earlier interview. Of course, you may use confidential information when you report on your research. It was given to you for that purpose. But you must present it in such a way that the source cannot be recognized, even by your instructor, who may be better versed than you imagine in the politics of your community. He has perhaps in earlier years read other student papers about the same town or ward. All these are elementary precautions which you must take for the sake of preserving your own personal honor and for the sake of students and social scientists who will come after you.

Merely because you have not explicitly promised to keep confidence, you do not thereby have permission to repeat your informants' conversation. In many interviews a tacit understanding of secrecy develops. That too you must respect as much as an explicit promise. Certainly informants who adopt a confidential manner and who, even of their own volition and without assurances of secrecy, tell you intimate details of politics will feel deeply wronged if you repeat their words. That you made no definite promise of secrecy will not lessen their resentment.

CHAPTER VI

Conducting the Interview

While interviewing has become a basic tool of the social sciences and as such has been discussed extensively, the particular kind of interviewing necessary for research on politics has been practiced less than others and has, therefore, seldom been written about. The only comments directly in point are in Alexander Heard's essay, "Interviewing Southern Politicians," which appeared in Volume 44 of the *American Political Science Review* (December, 1950), pp. 886-96. Somewhat less directly in point, but nevertheless valuable as an account of interviewing persons of stature and consequence in the national community, is Lewis Anthony Dexter, "Role Relationships and Conceptions of Neutrality in Interviewing," *American Journal of Sociology,* Vol. 62 (1956), pp. 153-57. These excellent essays are, however, intended less as advice for students than as reports on the tools of research projects. The paucity of printed material on this kind of interviewing is what necessitates this manual.

The assertion about the paucity of material on interviewing in political research may strike some political scientists as surprising. It is true that there are a number of interviewing manuals. Besides those mentioned elsewhere in this chapter, a number of outstanding manuals, some of which have gone through many editions, should perhaps be listed here:

W. V. Bingham and B. V. Moore, *How to Interview* (3rd edition, New York, Harper and Brothers, 1941)

Robert L. Kahn and Charles F. Cannel, *The Dynamics of Interviewing: Theory, Technique, and Cases* (New York, John Wiley and Sons, 1957)

Robert K. Merton, Marjorie Fiske, and Patricia Kendall, *The Focussed Interview: A Manual* (3rd edition, Glencoe, Illinois, The Free Press, 1956).

Stanley L. Payne, *The Art of Asking Questions* (Princeton, Princeton University Press, 1951)

Pauline Young, *Interviewing in Social Work: A Sociological Analysis* (New York, McGraw-Hill, 1935)

In addition, the entire issue of the *American Journal of Sociology* for September, 1956, is devoted to essays on the technique of interviewing. All this material is, however, largely irrelevant to the problem of interviewing in research on politics. Most of the writing about interviewing concerns situations in which the interviewer is the social superior or at least the social equal of the respondent. But the investigator, especially the student investigator, in politics is likely to be, or to be considered, the social and professional inferior of the person he is questioning. In Merton, *et al., The Focussed Interview* (p. 178 of the 2nd edition, New York, Bureau of Applied Social Research, Columbia University, 1952) it is remarked: "In any interview situation, even when the maximum of rapport has been established, there is, necessarily, some latent feeling on the part of the interviewees that they are dominated by the interviewer." This is undoubtedly true of interviewing in research on primitive society or low socio-economic groups in the United States, in psychotherapy or medical practice, counselling and social work, police and courtroom practice, and even public opinion polling (which is what *The Focussed Interview* concerns). In some instances, such as opinion research or the work of Kinsey and Roethlisberger, the main problem is to minimize the interviewer's dominance (Payne's work, just cited, and Herbert H. Hyman *et al.*, *Interviewing in Social Research: A Systematic Analysis of Sources of Error in the Personal Interview*, Chicago, University of Chicago Press, 1954 are both devoted to the problem of minimization); in other instances, such as courtroom practice and some kinds of psychotherapy, the problem is to exploit and maximize the interviewer's dominance. But in research on politics one can neither maximize nor minimize interviewer's dominance for it is often, usually even, the respondent who is dominant. The interviewer is in the position of a petitioner for information. Hence the considerable detail on the techniques of interviewing set forth in this Study is intended to fill real lacunae in the literature and to satisfy the needs of political scientists who want to interview, not human guinea pigs, but men of local importance who can tell them significant facts.

From the point of view of the method by which conducted, interviews may be classified as directed and non-directed. *The directed interview is* characterized by the fact that the interviewer, in search of specific information, asks a series of specific questions. When he receives an answer, often a one word answer, he goes on to the next question and does not allow the informant to wander away from the topics on which the interviewer seeks information. Public-opinion poll takers are well-known practitioners of this kind of interviewing, as are Dr. Kinsey and his associates.

Excellent discussions of the practical aspects of conducting directed interviews may be found in:

Marie Jahoda, Morton Deutsch, and Stuart W. Cook, *Research Methods in Social Relations* (2 vols., New York, Dryden Press, 1951), Vol. 1, pp. 151-208.

Paul B. Sheatsley, "The Art of Interviewing and a Guide to Interviewer Selection and Training," in Jahoda, Deutsch, and Cook, *op. cit.,* Vol. 2, pp. 463-92.

Alfred C. Kinsey, Wardell B. Pomeroy, and Clyde E. Martin, *Sexual Behavior in the Human Male* (Philadelphia, W. B. Saunders Co., 1948), pp. 35-62.

The non-directed interview is characterized by the fact that the interviewer, putting just enough questions to keep the conversation alive and reasonably relevant, allows the informant to talk about whatever he (the informant) thinks important. This kind of interviewing was invented, as is well known, by Sigmund Freud. It has been used extensively in clinical psychology (by nearly all schools of psychologists and psychiatrists as well as by psychoanalysts), in research in business management, and in sociological and anthropological research. Its most extreme version is that of the anthropologist who lives in a primitive society for a year or two, simply listening and observing and recording what he sees and hears.

Excellent discussions of the practical aspects of conducting non-directed interviews may be found in:

Bronislaw Malinowski, *Argonauts of the Western Pacific* (London, G. Routledge and Sons, 1932), pp. 4-25. This is one of the most important and influential of the discussions of anthropological field methods. While it is not strictly relevant to political research, it contains a number of hints about devices for eliciting information from informants.

William Foote Whyte, "Observational Field-Work Methods," in Jahoda, Deutsch, and Cook, *op. cit.,* Vol. 2, pp. 293-313. Although this essay, in which one of the most sensitive of contemporary sociologists discusses his experiences in collecting material for *Street Corner Society* (cf. Appendix I-B), deals with a deeper kind of interviewing than you can undertake, some of his problems are nevertheless related to yours.

F. J. Roethlisberger and William J. Dickson, *Management and the Worker* (Cambridge, Massachusetts, Harvard University Press, 1939); pp. 293-310 contain full transcriptions of several interviews. The purpose of this interviewing was not to find out facts but to discover the subjective irritations of the employees of the Western Electric Company. Still, the actual interviews may suggest ways of proceeding with your own work.

Benjamin D. Paul, "Interviewing Techniques and Field Relationships," in A. L. Kroeber, editor, *Anthropology Today: An Encyclopedic Inventory* (Chicago, University of Chicago Press, 1953), pp. 430-51. This essay comments on field method in anthropology. While hardly pertinent to your problems, the essay concludes with a fairly exhaustive bibliography (pp. 449-51) on the interviewing technique.

In the interviews connected with this research you have two purposes. First, you want to obtain facts about events and political habits; for this purpose you need a directed interview. Second, you want to absorb some of the atmosphere of local politics and thereby to interpret local traditions; for this purpose you need a non-directed interview. Since your interviews will rarely exceed an hour or two in length, you must in that short time achieve a judicious combination of the directed and non-directed interview. It is to help you achieve that balance that this chapter is written.

An interview is said to be directed when the interviewer controls the time and content of the interview by asking questions. Since you have a number of quite specific questions to ask, you can control the course of the interview by the simple process of putting questions. Generally speaking, the more rapidly the questions are put, the briefer and more relevant the answers. If, in the study of a particular event, you devise some quite specific questions, it is wise to have them well enough in mind to be able to put them in quick succession. For professional rapidity it is helpful to jot down key words of the questions on a small sheet of paper, which can aid memory during the conversation. Reference to it will enable you to control the tempo of the questioning.

Interviewing in research on politics probably should not be entirely of the directed sort. The problem is how to obtain a non-directed interview on the subjects that interest you, that is, how to obtain reminiscence about local affairs rather than a tirade on national issues. In most instances, the solution to this problem is to start with a directed interview and then allow it to slip gradually into a non-directed one, when the informant shows an inclination to reminisce or to generalize on appropriate subjects. You run the risk of irrelevant garrulity, of course; but you may also learn much that direct questioning can never reveal. Once you have decided to let your informant control the content of the interview, your only obligation is to keep him talking. This you can do in several ways. At appropriate intervals you can insert meaningless but encouraging interjections, "How interesting!" "That's surprising!" "Why?" etc. Or you can, if the conversation lags, ask a very general question. Or, probably with most effect, you can simply keep silent. If the interview has been fairly animated and your informant has been interested in talking to you, your silence will probably keep him talking. Most people are embarrassed by a sudden silence in a theretofore animated conversation and feel obligated to break it. If you do not do so, your informant in all likelihood will. And in his eagerness he will often tell you things he might otherwise have kept to himself.

The interviewer who has mastered his art does not, of course, follow a rigid division of the conversation into directed and non-directed parts. Rather, starting with a directed interview, he may allow it to slip into a non-directed one, regain control, and then again allow the informant to control, perhaps repeating this latter process several times. In seeking to regain control, however, it is especially important not to interrupt. Roethlisberger and Dickson comment wisely on this point:

> The attitude of the interviewer [in a non-directed interview] should be one of patiently listening to what the speaker has to say before making any comment himself. He should listen and not talk until the person has made a complete statement. Probably the quickest way to stop a person from sufficiently expressing himself is to interrupt. No matter how irrelevant the material may seem to the interviewer, he must remember that the person being interviewed probably cannot easily state what is really important to him.*

In brief, the central advice of this chapter is this: To direct the interview, you need a ready supply of specific questions. To force your informant to direct it, you need a ready supply of ejaculatory platitudes, general questions, and an attitude of attentive silence.

Such are the general methods of conducting an interview. In addition there are a number of rules of thumb on which experienced interviewers largely agree and to which you will do well to adhere:

1. *In the directed portion of the interview, ask only one question at a time.* Do not ask, for example, "How much money did you collect and did you put in any money of your own?" Such a question confuses the informant. Although attempting to answer quite honestly, he may answer: "I used $750." You may infer from this that he had a total of $750, when, in fact, what he meant was that he had $750 of his own money in addition to what he collected from supporters. Another difficulty with such a question is that it allows the informant to ignore part of your question. He may well answer at length that he put in $750 of his own money, that it was very difficult for him to do so, that there ought to be some better way of financing politics,

* F. J. Roethlisberger and William J. Dickson, *Management and the Worker* (Cambridge, Mass., Harvard University Press, 1939), p. 287.

that the personal expense is what keeps good people from running for office, and that his rich opponent could afford to outspend him. By then he is out of breath and you may want to seize the opportunity to ask if he can estimate how much his opponent spent—a good question for it will provide a check on the opponent's answer when you interview him. And when this latter question has been answered, you are so far from the subject of your informant's total campaign fund that it is embarrassing to return to it, especially if he has shown reluctance. Thus you may never learn that he was given $2200 by his friends.

2. *In the directed portion of the interview, if you have questions that you believe may prove embarrassing to your informant, wait until you have established a friendly atmosphere and until an opportunity presents itself.* An embarrassing question early in the interview may utterly destroy rapport and vitiate the interview. For example, if you wish to ask an unsuccessful candidate why he committed a serious blunder during the campaign—why, perhaps, he challenged his opponent to a debate when his opponent was a much more skillful and effective debater—it is best to wait until the informant has introduced the subject of the debate himself. Then you can, naturally and without impropriety, ask your question. If your informant never himself mentions his blunder, you can bring it up, but only after you have established rapport. Even then, however, it is best to approach the subject indirectly, by asking, for example, what he considers the highlights of the campaign. If he mentions the debate, you have an opportunity to question him about it. If, however, he chooses to ignore his blunder, you can remark that you had heard of the debate and that you suppose he would include it in his list of highlights. Should he reply, "Oh, yes, of course," you can quite naturally inquire into his motives for suggesting the debate. Should he reply, "No, I don't think so," it is appropriate to pursue the reasons for his negative answer

and, in the course of that pursuit, much will be revealed about his blunder.

3. *Throughout the interview it is especially important to display a sympathetic interest in your informant and what he is talking about.* Friendliness is reciprocal; you cannot expect sympathetic interest unless you extend it. Indeed, unless you are interested, really interested, in what your informant has to say, he will quickly sense your boredom and probably terminate the interview. The interest you display must be genuine, for simulated interest is as apparent to most people as frank boredom.

You can display your own friendliness early in the interview by thanking your informant for giving you some of his time and by showing your respect for his position. Throughout the interview, you ought occasionally to express your interest by smiling, nodding, etc., and by interjections like: "Oh, I think that's very interesting," "Why that is a fascinating point," "I never thought of that," etc. Such comments, uttered with sincerity, will help maintain a friendly atmosphere throughout the interview. Some of you will perhaps feel that such comments are simply "buttering up" and hence an offense to your dignity. If they are feigned, they are indeed an offense. If they are sincere, however, they are simply politeness, natural to any gracious person.

At the same time as you consciously attempt to create sympathy, you must not destroy it by unconscious expressions of disapproval. The authors of the Kinsey report, who are doubtless the most experienced interviewers in the United States, have some wise observations to make on this point:

> The sympathetic interviewer records his reaction in ways that may not involve spoken words but which are, nonetheless, readily comprehended by most people. A minute change of a facial expression, a slight tensing of a muscle, a flick of an eye, a trace of a change in one's voice, a slight inflection

> or change in emphasis, slight changes in one's rate of speaking, slight hesitancies in putting a question or in following up with the next question, one's choice of words, one's spontaneity in inquiring about items that are off the usual routine, or any of a dozen and one other involuntary reactions betray the interviewer's emotions, and most subjects quickly understand them. . . .
>
> If the interviewer's manner spells surprise, disapproval, condemnation, or even cold disinterest, he will not get the whole of the record. If his reactions add up right, then the subject is willing to tell his story. The interview has become an opportunity for him to develop his own thinking.*

These comments grow out of interviewing on a more personal and intimate subject than politics; but they apply to politics also and you would do well to heed them.

4. *In no instance should you argue with an informant.* All those who have written about interviewing are agreed that one of the easiest ways to destroy rapport is to indicate disapproval. Argument is, of course, an extreme form of disapproval. Furthermore, since in most instances student interviewers are some years younger than the informants, argument becomes a kind of impudence. In this situation, argument not only destroys rapport, it also generates a positive hostility. Occasionally you may interview a person who, despite the difference in age, treats you as his equal and trades interpretations of local politics with you. When this occurs, if it ever does, it is of course admissible to disagree and to offer alternative points of view. But, even in this unusual circumstance, it is probably unwise and impolite to attempt refutation of your informant's position.

* Kinsey, Pomeroy, and Martin, *op. cit.*, p. 42.

CHAPTER VII

Recording the Interview

There are two schools of thought on the question of whether or not notes should be taken during the course of the interview. One school holds that recording has the effect of frightening the informant. Most people, so the argument runs, tend to withhold information if they see it written down. William Foote Whyte remarks in this connection: "Outside the laboratory, it seems to me impossible for the observer to take notes on the spot without destroying the spontaneity of the relationship." * On the basis of this theory Alexander Heard took no notes when he interviewed Southern politicians for "to do so would have de-

* William Foote Whyte, "Observational Field Work Methods," in Marie Jahoda, Morton Deutsch, and Stuart W. Cook, *Research Methods in Social Relations: With Especial Reference to Prejudice* (2 vols., New York, Dryden, 1951), p. 504.

feated the effort to create a conversational atmosphere." Instead, he went to his car after each interview and dictated memoranda on an Ediphone, averaging about ten pages for each interview. (The interviews varied from fifteen minutes to half a day.)

The other school of thought holds that note-taking during the interview is necessary to get an accurate record. Those who have followed this procedure insist that note-taking does not materially affect rapport. Such was the experience of interviewers in what are probably the two most extensive interviewing projects ever undertaken in this country. At the Western Electric Company Hawthorne Works in the 1930's the Harvard Business School interviewers were instructed to take as nearly as possible verbatim notes in shorthand. Roethlisberger and Dickson remark: "At first it was thought that taking notes might make the employee reluctant to talk, but it was found that this was not true." * Similarly the authors of the Kinsey report comment:

> It has been said that there is a loss of rapport when the interviewer records during the interview. For these reasons we attempted to follow standard practice [i.e., not recording during the interview] early in this study and found that it introduced a tremendous error into the records. . . . After the first few months of this study, we began to record all of the data directly in the presence of the subject, and there has been no indication that this has been responsible for any loss of rapport or interference with the subject's free exposure of confidences.

They then go on to comment that the occasion for the loss of rapport is not note-taking, but instead obtrusive and inept note-taking:

> We have become convinced that any loss of rapport which comes when data are recorded directly has been consequent upon the longhand method of writing out answers while the

* Roethlisberger and Dickson, *op. cit.*, p. 193.

> subject sits in silence waiting for the next question. This is the thing that is destructive to rapport. By using a code for recording, it has been possible in the present study to record as rapidly as one can carry on a conversation, without loss of rapport or blockage on the subject's part.*

This last observation suggests a reconciliation between the two points of view. It is probably quite certain that nearly any informant will hesitate and perhaps even stop talking if you sit stooped over your paper laboriously recording each word he utters. When you are so zealously engaged in recording, your informant will have the impression that he is talking to a tape recorder rather than a person. Conversation becomes a hesitant monologue and rapport is lost. On the other hand, rapport is seldom destroyed by taking a few unobtrusive notes, especially if you jot them down without directing your eyes away from your informant.

Disagreement among professional interviewers over note-taking during an interview comes in part from a difference in purpose. The Harvard interviewers at Western Electric were especially interested in discovering nuances in words and phrasing, nuances from which they could infer the existence of an informant's obsessive thinking. For such delicate interpretation they needed nearly verbatim records. Dr. Kinsey and his associates sought for the most part to obtain brief (often numerical) answers to an average of three hundred questions. Even very carefully trained memories cannot normally recall every answer accurately an hour or so later. On the other hand, Alexander Heard was interested in gross outlines of events, descriptions of campaign techniques, etc.—all of which an experienced interviewer can recall without difficulty. Thus, those who want an exact record of sentences find note-taking indispensable while those who want simply the facts contained in sentences can delay recording until after the interview.

* Kinsey, Pomeroy, and Martin, *op. cit.*, p. 50.

Considering the purpose of this research, it is probably wisest for you to take some notes. You are not experienced interviewers who have trained yourselves to recall whole conversations, exchange by exchange. For the sake of accuracy and completeness, therefore, you ought to record some specific facts and sentences. On the other hand, you ought not to take notes obtrusively—certainly not in the way you take notes in the classroom. Classroom notes are usually intended to aid memory as much as three or four months after they are taken. Interview notes are intended to aid memory only for an hour or so after the interview.

It is possible to take notes quite unobtrusively in the following way: Early in the conversation ask a question whose answer you might reasonably be expected to write down—"What public offices have you held?" "Where can I get in touch with your campaign manager?" etc. As your informant answers, draw a 3 by 5 inch file card (or a small notebook) and a *short* pencil from your pocket or purse. These are unobtrusive materials, especially if the pencil is short. (Descriptions of journalists at work often poke fun at their habit of using stubby pencils. But stubby pencils are a trick of the trade, not simply blasé carelessness, as the humorists would have them.) Once you have brought cards and pencil into the open to record a particular answer, you can then occasionally jot down a key word. Very few informants will be bothered by this kind of note-taking. The use of such materials in recording has another advantage: If you have entered a list of the key words of your proposed questions on the same card, it can be used to aid memory both during and after the interview.

Notes taken by this suggested method of recording the interview will probably mean nothing in a short time, even so little as a week later. You must, therefore, expand these notes soon after the interview, preferably immediately after. Alexander Heard went immediately to his automobile where he dictated a record. Most psychiatrists dictate a record immediately after the patient has left. You, likewise, can extend your notes in an automobile or at a drugstore lunch counter or at a hotel lobby. Immediately after an interview, it is possible to write out, with the aid of a few jottings, the give and take of a conversation and to record at least the striking sentences verbatim. But the memory of the flow of a conversation and of particular sentences fades quickly, usually in less than an hour.

The record of each interview ought to be fairly extensive. A rule of thumb, which is, of course, applicable only when you have had a profitable interview, is to spend about as much time to write out a record in longhand as it took to conduct the interview. The record ought to contain the following items:

1. a statement about the character of your informant as revealed in his remarks. If he has indicated anything about his education, religion, financial status, etc., record this. Be especially careful to record those details of the conversation which indicated that he did or did not understand the issues and politics of the community.
2. as complete a record of the conversation as you can recall
3. a list of the items discovered in the interview that seem to deserve investigation elsewhere

and, perhaps most important of all

4. your reactions about the validity of the comments; for example, whether or not your informant's tone of voice conveyed the suggestion that he was boasting or confessing or telling the truth

Finally, if you have undertaken to describe by means of a long series of interviews a fairly complex event, you ought to prepare a preliminary chronology which you edit, alter, add to, etc., after each interview. Incidentally, gaps in this chronology will suggest questions for subsequent interviews.

CHAPTER VIII

Observation Methods

Interviewing may be extended in length until it becomes a continuous survey of political behavior over a substantial period of time. Thereby its character is changed and this new thing we call, for lack of a better name, *observation.*

Two kinds of observation must be distinguished at the outset. One is repeated and detailed public-opinion interviewing of one group of subjects over a fairly long period of time. The classic examples of this sort of observation are the study of Presidential campaigns in Sandusky, Ohio, and Elmira, New York, reported respectively in Paul Lazarsfeld, *et al., The People's Choice,* and Bernard Berelson, *et al., Voting* (See Appendix I-A). By its very nature, however, such observation requires many persons and much money. Naturally, also, the technical details of organizing and planning and executing so extended a survey are highly complex. Undergraduates cannot, therefore, independently conduct this kind of observation. Hence, further discussion is omitted here.

A second kind of observation is essentially similar to the field techniques of the anthropologist or sociologist who lives for months or even years with his subjects in order to collect as much material as is humanly possible about the details of their behavior. He conducts what might be described as a continuous non-directed interview, with occasional interludes of directed interviewing. The great advantage of this method over simple interviewing is, of course, that it yields more information and makes possible frequent and elaborate crosschecks to determine the accuracy of informants' assertions. Unfortunately, a method that works so well for understanding and describing primitive societies or groups of inferior social status in the United States cannot be transferred without change to the study of American politics. The great advantage that an anthropologist studying Melanesian society or a sociologist studying a Boston slum have over a political scientist studying community leaders is that the anthropologist and the sociologist have a higher social status than the people they study. Hence the informants at least tolerate constant observation and interminable questions about what are often private matters. It is not to be expected that American politicians, who are often the social as well as political leaders of their communities, will tolerate such extensive intrusion into their private business, especially when the intruder is an adolescent, whose family is perhaps of lower social status than their own.

Nevertheless, with appropriate adjustments, somewhat similar techniques of observation can be used. These adjusted techniques are discussed in this chapter.

It is often possible for students to offer their services to politicians. During a campaign, for example, political parties are desperately in need of help in a variety of ways. Students can give this help and thereby obtain a post for almost continuous observation of a campaign, after the fashion of the anthropologist. But here a word of caution is necessary. Sometimes teachers of political science have arranged for students to serve parties or candidates in just this way, with results that have often been far from pleasing either to the students or to the politicians. Typically, the process of failure has gone something like this: After the teacher has arranged for the service, the student shows up at party headquarters. The campaign manager or some such person receives him with a few noncommittal and conventionally kind words and then introduces him to a secretary in the office. She gives him a pile of circulars and envelopes and abruptly instructs him to spend the next three days stuffing one into the other. The student, by now just a little offended by the lack of appreciation of his status as a sophomore, but nevertheless eager to observe successfully, falls to with a will and busily stuffs envelopes for fully three-quarters of an hour. Then he begins to think up reasons why he should go back to the college. Finally he announces that he has to go study for an economics quiz and that he will be back tomorrow at one P.M. Sometimes he goes back and sometimes he doesn't; but in any event the observation was a failure.

Who is the culprit here? One can hardly blame the student for his boredom, especially when he knows he is learning and contributing very little. Neither can one blame the overburdened secretary who wants to clear up some of her overdue work. And finally one cannot blame the campaign manager who is naturally a little dubious about turning over significant duties to an inexperienced young stranger. Actually, the culprit is not a person but a situation. The enterprise breaks down over the mutual failure of the campaign manager and the instructor to find the student some work, however lowly, that permits him to observe. And so we can formulate this general rule: Simply helping a political party organization is not necessarily a satisfactory way of observing politics. Rather, the help must be given in a situation that allows the student at least a glimpse of political behavior on the decision-making level. If this rule is not followed, so-called observation of politics may easily degenerate into simple performance of the almost limitless clerical routine of contemporary politics.

To help in the application of this rule, I offer the following list of what seem to me to be good observation posts for students:

1. Candidates whose election district is territorially large must travel continuously, especially in the latter part of a campaign. A student, or perhaps a team of students, can serve as chauffeurs, an ideal post for observation. Energetic candidates often use their traveling time to dictate speeches, instructions to associates, and letters. Or they may have strategy discussions with campaign aides. They may even actually talk to the student chauffeur. This observation is admittedly a kind of eavesdropping; but it does not violate the canons of good taste so long as the candidate knows what the student is doing and is permitted to read over whatever the student eventually writes.

2. Occasionally parties or individual candidates conduct opinion polls as a device to discover (a) their chance of winning and (b) the appeal of various features of their public argument. If a group of students, perhaps with the advice and help of an instructor, can do this polling, there is an unusual opportunity for observation. The polling itself is, of course, drudgery and must not be confused with observation unless it is technically on at least as advanced a level as that done in Elmira in 1948. But there are other rewards: Planning the sample to be polled provides an excellent introduction to polling techniques. Much more importantly, however, planning the questions to be asked, a job which must be done with a party chairman or a candidate or a campaign manager, allows students to catch a glimpse (perhaps even a several hour glimpse) of some of the elements of decision-making at the highest level. All the important considerations of the campaign (program emphasis, ethnic appeal, timing of issues and effort, etc.,

etc.) must enter into the discussion at such a session. The chance for observation of such discussions of grand strategy is worth all the rather dull drudgery of polling.

3. Occasionally a campaign manager or even a candidate will, if asked, allow a student to travel about with him. sometimes for a day or so, sometimes for even longer. This is an invaluable opportunity for it permits prolonged and repeated interviewing on the basis of events occurring at the moment. (I might add that this kind of observation is not so rare as it may seem. Students of mine have occasionally been offered this opportunity even when they have not sought it.)

4. Between campaigns, political party offices sometimes need help in what they call research, which is usually gathering numerical data about voters. The content of this so-called research is, of course, largely useless from an educational point of view. It is even a worse chore than public-opinion polling. But, as in the case of opinion polling, the labor is worthwhile if the student is permitted to engage in the discussions in which the research is planned. Here again considerations of grand strategy must be discussed openly. If students are not permitted to participate in planning the "research," however, the project is probably of one-sided value, all for the party and little for the student.

5. Finally it is to be noted that even the drudgery of stuffing envelopes is not to be despised if it leads to access to the main figures of a campaign. The proviso is important. Sometimes the drudgery leads only to more drudgery, especially if the student is shy and the campaign hectic. But if the people in the office gradually take the student into their confidence, then the drudgery has opened up an observation post. In such cases as this, the question always is: Is the drudgery worth the prospect? My general impression is that in a small office the drudgery eventually pays off if the student is both affable and enthusiastic, while in a large office it hardly ever does regardless of the personality of the student.

It is often impossible for students to obtain observation posts of the sort just listed. This fact need not foreclose observation, however. One kind of fairly impersonal observation, possible at least in areas in which a heated campaign is in progress, is what might be called journalistic observation. A student or, better, a group of students sharing the duty and jointly interpreting the results, can cover *every* meeting or other public activity (television and radio appearances, plant-gate or street-corner handshaking, etc.) as if they were journalists. Such activity does not provide an opportunity for interpreting all aspects of the candidate's behavior unless, of course, it is accompanied by extensive interviewing; but it does allow students to make a complete record of the whole course of the public campaign.

All the kinds of observation previously listed assume that local politics is synonymous with election campaigns. This is, of course, very false. What officials do after they are elected is just as much a part of politics as is the process of getting elected. And some of this can be observed too, although the process of observation is a little more difficult and indeed haphazard. One place in particular in which the politics of local administration can be publicly observed is in the deliberations of a city council or a county board. Ordinarily such meetings are inordinately dull. Reports from the street committee, the public health committee, etc., are read and then unanimously approved (or approved perhaps with the dissenting vote of one crackpot). The reason for the superficial unanimity is, of course, that all the conflicts of interest are worked out in committee. But occasionally conflicts are not worked out beforehand and genuine disagreement spills out onto the floor. This you can investigate. Systematic interviewing of all the members of the council about why they voted the way they did almost certainly will uncover a few councilmen who blurt out (in anger or amusement) some of the genuine considerations involved on both sides. This suggests, then, an interesting and often rewarding kind of observation for a student (in a small town) or a group of students in a medium sized town: Visit the council meetings regularly, mastering your boredom in the hope of coming across the kind of conflict you can observe. The regularity of the visits is important, especially in smaller cities and counties where ordinarily council or board meetings have few visitors. After one or two meetings, the councilmen will become accustomed to your presence and forget any inhibitions occasioned by it. When an issue comes up that arouses genuine conflict, revealed perhaps by a roll-call vote with a fairly close margin between the majority and the minority, you have your cue to start probing with interviews. You can expect to discover a fairly exact picture of the influences behind a particular political decision. This is more than many semi-professional politicians ever achieve in their entire careers. But a note of warning: Do not pick out conflicts that involve really basic community policies (such as major construction that requires a bond issue). Customarily the decisions in such conflicts take considerably longer than a college semester. Since you do not have unlimited time, study a conflict on a lower level, such as one over an item in a regular annual appropriation, that must be decided promptly.

All the observation in the world is useless, however, unless you have some definite principles about what to look for. Not all you see is relevant to politics. You must pick and choose among the events impinging on you. Once you start to pick and choose, you need a standard to choose by. What should you look for and what should you record? This is an extremely important and difficult question which you probably cannot begin to answer adequately until you have taken a number of courses in political science. To answer it fully here would require the exposition of a whole theory of politics. But I shall list some of the things which seem to me especially important and which are, I believe, within the powers of observation of even a novice:

1. Whom does the candidate see? A student chauffeur or a student who is invited to travel with a figure in a campaign has an excellent opportunity to observe this simple fact. If you can also discover what was discussed in the interviews between the candidate and various third parties, so much the better, although, of course, you dare not pry lest you destroy your entree. But even if you only rarely learn what was discussed, you can at least learn, from the list of persons seen, the following: (a) the kinds of voters to whom he makes a special appeal; (b) the kinds of persons whom he considers influential; and (c) the kind of person on whom he relies for help. It is often said that a campaign is the construction of a winning coalition; and you can often describe either what is a winning coalition or what the candidate thinks will be a winning coalition from the list of persons he sees. It is also often said that politics is concerned with who gets what, and you can often infer a considerable amount about the distribution if you know whom the candidate sees. Finally, it is often said of politics that "he who pays the piper calls the tune"; and sometimes you can discover from this list not only who pays the piper but also what tune is called.

2. What is the character of the candidate and the persons around him? Try to discover the candidate's value system as revealed in his behavior. What does he think is important? What is his picture of himself and his role in society? These are questions that can often be answered by inference from a twist of phrase or an apparently irrelevant and unimportant remark. They are, however, highly significant for understanding a particular event. When generalized, they are significant for understanding our politics. Consider the following specific question: Does the person you are observing try to force his ideological convictions on other people or does he tend to compromise his previously expressed opinions in conversation? In what kind of situations does he force opinions and in what kind does he compromise? It has often been suggested that candidates

are typically compromisers, that they try to impress their personalities but not their opinions on other people, while party functionaries, it is also said, are typically ideologists, trying to influence the opinions of other people. I know of no good evidence one way or another on this conjecture; but it is interesting to discover if it is true or false in particular cases.

Here is a note of warning: In the investigation of the character of candidates and the men around them do not allow yourself to become excessively concerned with backstairs gossip. In the Hanoverian era there was a rash of history books about backstairs gossip, based of course on the assumption that the course of public events was controlled by the course of love affairs among the great. Perhaps this assumption was true then, although I doubt it; it may even be rarely true now; but generally such material is almost wholly irrelevant to politics and should not be emphasized in your observation.

3. What roles does the candidate play? Each of us plays a role in our relationship with another person, that is, we behave toward the other one as we think we ought to behave in accordance with a mental picture we have of the relationship. With different people the role we play varies. You, as students, behave in one way toward your parents, in another way toward your teachers, in another way toward friends of the same sex, in another way toward friends of the opposite sex, in another way toward little children, etc. Doubtless, with some serious introspection, you could describe the roles you yourself play. With luck and good observation you can do something vastly more important and difficult: You can describe the roles somebody else plays, somebody society generally considers more significant than you.

All the foregoing questions can be answered only by extended and fairly intimate observation—although occasionally students of mine have been able to go pretty far in answering items (2) and (3) on the basis of two or three interviews. There are other and equally important questions, however, that can be answered from even the most impersonal observation:

4. Questions that can be answered about a campaign that has been observed in detail: What is the ideological and social basis of the appeal each candidate made to the voters? What kinds of voters did the candidates make a special effort to impress? Can you infer why? If there were ideological issues, how did the candidates develop their campaigns? If there were no apparent policy issues, how did each candidate attempt to differentiate his personality from his opponent's? How did the candidates attempt to arouse the interest of the voters? etc.

5. Questions that can be answered about the outcome of an observed legislative decision: Which community leaders in or out of politics seemed to have most influence on the observed outcome? What are the community traditions and prejudices that contributed to the outcome? What are the apparently unique or accidental circumstances that influenced the outcome?

* * *

Finally, I conclude this chapter with several comments about the technical methods of observation.

A fundamental rule that should never be violated is that the observed be aware of the fact and intention of the observation. That is, they must not be allowed to assume that the student is merely a volunteer helper without an academic interest. If this rule is not followed, your behavior becomes mere eavesdropping and snooping and loses its academic justification. An extension of this rule is that the major persons you observe should understand that they will be allowed to view your finished product. Without this assurance at the base of the relationship, you cannot expect to achieve rapport.

A second rule for extended observation is that the observer pick a party and candidate with whom he is, to some degree at least, sympathetic, personally or ideologically or both. In a brief interview you can perhaps hide disapproval and hostility successfully enough to create some rapport. But in extended observation you cannot possibly control your facial expressions, your incidental remarks, etc., that convey disapproval. Unless you are initially sympathetic to your informant, therefore, you are almost certain to reveal hostility toward him, and nothing more quickly destroys the rapport that is an absolute essential for extended observation.

A third rule for extended and intimate observation is that notebooks and pencils must resolutely be banished. In relatively brief interviews, these objects may be necessary; but in extended observation, where one has an opportunity to return again and again to a subject, notebooks are not needed and almost certainly destroy rapport.

Finally, a comment on student observers and political corruption: In extended observation students occasionally find themselves in the position of observing what appears to them to be illegal activity. What should be the student's action about this? As a primary rule, do not set about deliberately to discover evidence of illegalities. However romantic the role of the muckraking journalist may appear, remember that you are not professional law-enforcement officers and that you know little of what to look for and almost nothing of how to look for it. In short, you are likely to botch the job. Furthermore, if the persons whom you investigate discover what you are doing, they will, if they are innocent, be irreparably offended and you will have lost what might otherwise have been good informants. On the other hand, if they are guilty, it is not impossible that you may call forth physical retaliation on yourself.

But even without deliberate snooping, what seems to be evidence of corruption may come to you gratuitously. What then should you do? I suggest that first of all you discuss the matter with your instructor. What may seem to you to be illegal may in fact be merely a sharp practice not actually in violation of the law. Remember also that American politics is on the whole fairly honest, more honest certainly than journalistic stereotypes would lead one to believe. Sometimes student's imaginations, reinforced by the stereotypes, convert innocent politicking into a criminal conspiracy. If, however, in your instructor's opinion as well as your own, you have seen an illegality, the next question is: Do you have sufficient evidence to justify an indictment? If you don't, then you have not in a legal sense actually seen corruption, you have merely guessed at its existence. If, on the other hand, you and your instructor or both believe your evidence is sufficient for an indictment, you are, as a citizen, obligated to bring the matter to the attention of a prosecutor, preferably, of course, to the attention of a prosecutor who is not intimately associated politically with the persons whom you accuse.

CHAPTER IX

The Reliability of Information Obtained in Interviews and by Observation

One of the most impressive discoveries of psychology concerns the magnitude and extent of dissembling, distorting, concealing, and lying in daily conversations and daily life. Lawyers have long been aware that discovering truth in men is a rare and difficult thing. That is why they long ago developed exceedingly detailed and complicated rules of evidence. The rule that excludes hearsay evidence, for example, may be (as is often asserted today) excessively rigid, but it is based on the sure perception that gossip is seldom true. Unfortunately, lawyers' understanding of the pervasiveness of prevarication has never spread to the general public, which has instead discounted the lawyers' discovery, believing simply that a suit at law brings out the worst in men. Sigmund Freud deserves the credit for demonstrating to public satisfaction that all people regularly (though unconsciously) distort the history of their sex lives. While Freud believed that the unconscious dissembling occurred chiefly in one area of life, later psychologists found that it occurred in most areas. Public opinion poll takers, endeavoring to measure the amount of dissembling, have discovered that even on such simple questions as "Did you vote in [a recent and unimportant] election?" as many as 65 per cent of the informants replied untruthfully. Whether they did this consciously or unconsciously it is impossible to say.

The practical consequence of these discoveries is that in this generation we seldom take statements at their face value. Rather we try to discover why a particular statement is made, the interests that lie behind it, the distortions of reality it contains, etc. Hardly any of the investigations that use the interviewing technique have treated informants' statements as statements of fact about external events. For example, public opinion polls are, as their name implies, concerned with attitudes, which, if they deserve to be named facts at all, are facts about the informants' private mental lives. Other investigations impose even more severe limitations on the reliability of informants' statements. Interviewing at the Western Electric Company was undertaken not to discover objective facts about conditions of work in the factory, but to discover the workers' interpretations of the conditions, interpretations that were implicitly assumed to be false.

Our contemporary cynicism is not, however, wholly adequate. People do sometimes tell the exact truth. The fact that public opinion polls often predict election outcomes with fair accuracy is evidence of widespread truthfulness about voting intentions. We can assume therefore that people are truthful in other matters also. A few very important investigations have been conducted to learn facts from informants. Dr. Kinsey and his associates, for example, have been concerned with events, not opinions; and in that sense they can be said to trust informants to state facts. Anthropological and sociological investigations such as Malinowski's in the Trobriand Islands and Whyte's in the Boston slums, where the investigator lives for several years with the people whom he studies, are aimed at discovering facts about the society as well as the informants' interpretations. In them, informants are trusted to tell about other people as well as about themselves. And the interviews that led to V. O. Key's *Southern Politics* were conducted almost wholly to learn about events external to the informant. The interviewers largely ignored both personal opinion and personal facts.

All the studies mentioned in the previous paragraph have successfully brought to light important facts about our world. Their success, however, is a tribute less to the honesty of informants than to the wariness of interviewers. Anthropologists and sociologists have long since learned to cross-check all the information they gather. And cross-checking is possible when one is concerned with social events in which two or more people participate. Dr. Kinsey utilized the cross-check method whenever he could, but mostly he relied on checking the internal consistency of information gathered in an interview. The study of Southern politics was based on a mixture of interview reports and statistical analysis, which could to some degree be checked against each other.

Relying, as you must in the field study of politics, on informants who may or may not tell the exact truth, you must be cautious about accepting statements as fact. You must try to recognize both conscious and unconscious dissembling by your informants and you must develop procedures to penetrate beyond it. This chapter is intended to suggest some methods of recognition and penetration.

Unconscious dissembling occurs in many ways. The deepest and most pervasive sort arises because no person can comprehend the whole of events, because no person can order and arrange a complete picture of reality. And by reason of the insufficiency of his knowledge, each person is committed to a partial truth. This partiality is inherent in the human situation. You cannot hope to eradicate it from others or yourself. You can, however, attempt to minimize it by learning many facts. The more facts you draw into your consideration of a political event or situation, the less likely you are to fall prey to the cruder forms of bias in interpretation.

Besides this one great limitation on human understanding, there are simpler forms of dissembling which you can conceivably hope to penetrate. Many informants conveniently forget what they do not wish to remember. Many informants remember events in such a way that their personal and party interests appear in a favorable light. Many hide personal or party interests under statements about public interest, that is, they speak patriotically, but their patriotism is not so selfless as they imply. And finally, many adjust their statements of fact to what they believe appropriate for student ears. A county chairman who will quite frankly tell an adult interviewer how he collects campaign contributions from county employees may hesitate to reveal this socially disapproved practice to college sophomores. Conscious dissembling, such as concealing information detrimental to the informant or even outright lying, can occasionally be recognized from the manner of the speaker. Unconscious dissembling is more difficult to detect. You cannot expect to sense it from manner or tone for the person believes he is telling you the truth. Generally speaking, if either kind of dissembling can be recognized at all, it is by observing that the informant's story is inherently unrealistic or internally inconsistent or in conflict with statements made by other informants.

For example, politicians often accuse their opponents of dishonesty while maintaining their own purity. Such statements are inherently unrealistic. Almost invariably, if one party is dishonest in a community the other is dishonest also, for dishonesty is encouraged by example. It is very difficult, however, to penetrate such dissembling without rudeness or impudence. You can hardly ask a man if he is himself dishonest. On the other hand, when you think that an allegation of dishonesty is more than mere pique, you can at least ask for details and evidence. The details then offered may indicate as much about your informant as his opponent. They may also indicate that the allegation is mere gossip.

Internal inconsistencies can sometimes be straightened out by indirect questioning: Suppose an informant tells you at one point that the county leader promised to support him in the primary and then later on tells you that the county leader stayed neutral. The only way to accept both statements is to assume that the county leader broke faith with your informant. Yet, very few experienced politicians dishonor their word directly in such matters. It is, in the absence of other information, wiser to assume temporarily that your informant is dissembling. When the opportunity arises you might check on this particular inconsistency by, for example, asking the informant if he made his campaign plans on the basis of this promise or by asking why he thinks the county leader broke his word. Again, you can, when subsequently interviewing the county leader, ask him whether or not he ever contemplated supporting any candidate in the primary. (Note that questions of this sort must be carefully phrased so that you do not reveal to one informant what an earlier informant said of him.)

Conflicts among the statements of several informants must be submitted to cross-checking. For example, if opposing candidates state the issues facing the community in a recent election in significantly different terms, you can be almost certain that both are offering you rationalizations of which you ought properly to be skeptical. If, to give a specific example, the defeated candidate for mayor tells you that the main issue in the campaign was the high tax rate, while the re-elected incumbent tells you that the main issue was whether labor unions were going to take over the city government or a business administration was to be continued, you would hardly be justified in accepting either version. Instead you ought to try to ask questions that will throw more light on both statements. You might, for example, find out if the tax rate really is abnormally high in comparison with other cities of the same size and if there is a really large labor union membership in the community (large enough, when united, to win an election). If neither statement proves reasonable or true, ask yourself—and perhaps additional informants—what benefit accrued to each candidate to state the issue in these terms. To penetrate even one such rationalization by the device of cross-checking is a major achievement and you will learn much about local politics if you do so.

You may not have the opportunity or the occasion to penetrate dissembling. It is almost certain, however, that you will have to judge the reliability of gossip. Political gossip is a part of the daily life of every community. Alexander Heard, in the essay already quoted, remarks with some surprise on the prevalence of gossip.

> Even responsible citizens succumb to the temptation to repeat political gossip as though it were gospel. In every state the interviewer encountered questionable gossip that permeated the whole political community and was accepted by some experienced observers as reliable. He made a point of tracing some of this gossip to its source. Numbers of items were found to have originated in nothing more substantial than speculation in high quarters, or simply in a misquotation of an informed individual.*

In the traditional Anglo-American rules of evidence all gossip is, as hearsay evidence, inadmissible. And rightly so, for stories about events in which the witness was not per-

* Heard, *op. cit.*, p. 896.

sonally involved are almost never true in details and often are false in their entirety. Yet in some cases you may have to use gossip, if only for the leads it may give. And for that reason you will need to differentiate between that which is inherently false and that which you can inquire about further. Some gossip carries within itself the proof of its own falsity. For example, a story about what two persons said to each other in a private interview is on its face questionable for, if the conversation was really private, no third person could know about it. Therefore such gossip would never seem credible. Yet it is a common substance of political conversation. A classic example is the story, widely circulated during the 1944 campaign, that President Roosevelt in a private telephone conversation told Robert Hannegan, the Democratic national chairman: "Clear it [the Vice-Presidential nomination] with Sidney [Hillman, the chairman of the CIO Political Action Committee]." This bears all the earmarks of an invented story and did in fact greatly embarrass the journalist who first published it. (How, one asks, can a journalist know what was said in a private telephone conversation, especially when he is not able to interview the person at either end? Perhaps he tapped the phone, but this is both illegal and unlikely. One cannot avoid the impression that he made up the story to fill his daily column of political gossip with "inside" information.) Other gossip is not so easily discredited and ignored. Consider, for example, a persistent rumor that a ward leader of the minority party occasionally throws votes to candidates of the majority party in return for money or patronage. It is difficult to verify such rumors. One can attempt to discover evidence in election returns; for example, it may be noted that while ordinarily the candidates of the minority party receives 40 per cent of the votes in the ward, occasionally one receives only 10 per cent. But even this strange pattern is not evidence of a corrupt bargain. It may simply reflect the ward leader's indifference or hostility to the candidate of his own party. Indeed, the full investigation of such rumors is probably beyond the capacity of student researchers. Since they are an important part of the political life of the community, you may have to report them—but take care to report them as gossip, not as fact.

CHAPTER X

Statistical Methods of Testing Reliability

Many of the assertions commonly made about politics are partially subject to verification by statistical testing. It is desirable that you use such tests whenever possible, for statistical verification does to a certain degree eliminate the bias of both informants and observers. There is, of course, always the danger of error in the interpretation of statistical tests, too; but this danger is one of an easily identifiable error, while the danger of bias is not always identifiable at all. Unfortunately, desirable as statistical tests are, many college students are never introduced to the method of statistics and usually those who are do not receive the introduction until near the end of their college careers. Consequently they stand in somewhat unjustified awe of statistics and fear to use statistical tests, even though they often arrive at hypotheses that can be adequately tested only by the use of statistics. A brief and extraordinarily lucid introduction to statistics is fortunately available: V. O. Key, Jr., *A Primer of Statistics for Political Scientists* (see Appendix I-E). This work is simple enough so that the interested student can learn the basic elements of statistical methods from it even without formal instruction. What I will therefore attempt to do here is to give a brief example of the use of a statistical test and to suggest various kinds of hypotheses that are subject to statistical verification.

The following example of the verification of a hypothesis by a statistical test is adapted from the work of an undergraduate student of the author. After a preliminary survey of the politics of the community he was studying, the student decided to make an extensive study of a recent and hotly contested campaign for county judge. One of the elements of the campaign, he shortly discovered, had to do with the party affiliation or putative party affiliation of the candidates. Although the election was nonpartisan, most voters probably knew that one of the candidates, here called Candidate A, was a Democrat for he had been state chairman of the party and over the previous decade had always taken an active part in supporting the Democratic ticket in both the county and the state. The other candidate, here called Candidate B, attempted to keep his party affiliation secret; but, since his campaign manager was a well-known Republican leader and since most of his campaign workers were active in Republican politics, it was generally believed by those who took an interest in politics that the candidate himself was a Republican also. Naturally, some persons to whom the student talked asserted that these affiliations influenced the way people voted, that is, they asserted that Democrats voted for Candidate A and Republicans voted for Candidate B. Others, however, asserted that the party affiliation of the candidates had nothing to do with the voting. Good arguments could be presented on both sides. On the one hand, the evident association of both candidates with a political party would suggest that voters were influenced by partisan considerations. On the other hand, the fact that Candidate B, the Republican, won in a county that had for the past decade been turning in majorities as high as 60 per cent for Democratic candidates suggested that personal rather than partisan considerations influenced the voters.

The student wondered how to reconcile or rather to choose between these conflicting interpretations. On the basis of his own judgment of the relative perspicacity and honesty of his informants (who included both candidates and their campaign managers), he was inclined to believe that partisan considerations had indeed largely influenced the voting. But considering the difference of opinion among persons far more versed in the community's politics and far more mature in their judgment than he, he could hardly set himself up as an arbiter between these conflicting interpretations. Here, therefore, was an obvious place to attempt statistical verification. So he adopted the hypothesis that partisan considerations had largely influenced the voting. It was then necessary to find a way to test it.

The test he decided upon was a so-called correlation of the vote by precincts for Candidate A, the Democrat, with the vote in the same precincts for the Democratic candidate for Congress in the previous Congressional election. He reasoned that, if the correlation was fairly high, he could conclude that the hypothesis was verified. Otherwise, he would conclude that it was not. Incidentally, he chose the vote for Congressman, rather than for some other office, as the standard of party affiliation because he believed that in the last previous election many voters had been influenced in their vote for President, governor, and several county offices by personal rather than partisan considerations. This is a somewhat difficult point to prove, but some validity was lent to it by the fact that the Democratic candidates for representative, lieutenant governor, state treasurer, and attorney-general got about the same number of votes while the Democratic candidates for President and governor ran behind them and the Democratic candidates for county office ran ahead of them.

Having collected these returns he plotted them on a "scatter diagram," which is shown in Figure I. On the horizontal axis of the graph he measured the percentage of the total vote received by Candidate A. On the vertical axis he measured the percentage of the total vote received by the Democratic candidate for Congress in the last previous election. Then, he located each precinct in the county on this graph so that each dot represents the outcome of the two elections in each of the thirty precincts. The dot marked "Precinct A," for example, where Candidate A received 45 per cent of the total vote and where earlier the Democratic candidate for Congress received 41 per cent of the vote, is located at the intersection of a line perpendicular to the horizontal axis at 45 with a line perpendicular to the vertical axis at 41.

It is apparent from a brief inspection of the scatter diagram that, in general, as the Democratic Congressional candidate's percentage goes up so does Candidate A's percentage. On the basis of this diagram we can say that the two variables have a fairly high "positive correlation." (If all the dots had lain on a straight line slanting upward and to the right, we would say that the positive correlation was perfect, that is, that each move upward in one variable was accompanied by a similar move upward in the other. If, as could hardly be imagined in this case, all the dots had lain on a straight line slanting downward and to the right, we would say that a perfect negative correlation existed, that is, that each move upward in one variable was accompanied by a similar move downward in the other variable. If, as also can hardly be imagined in this case, all the dots had lain on a line parallel to either the horizontal or vertical axis, we would say that the correlation was zero, that is, that a movement in one variable was not accompanied at all by a movement in the other variable. There is a statistical measure of the degree by which a correlation varies through

FIGURE I

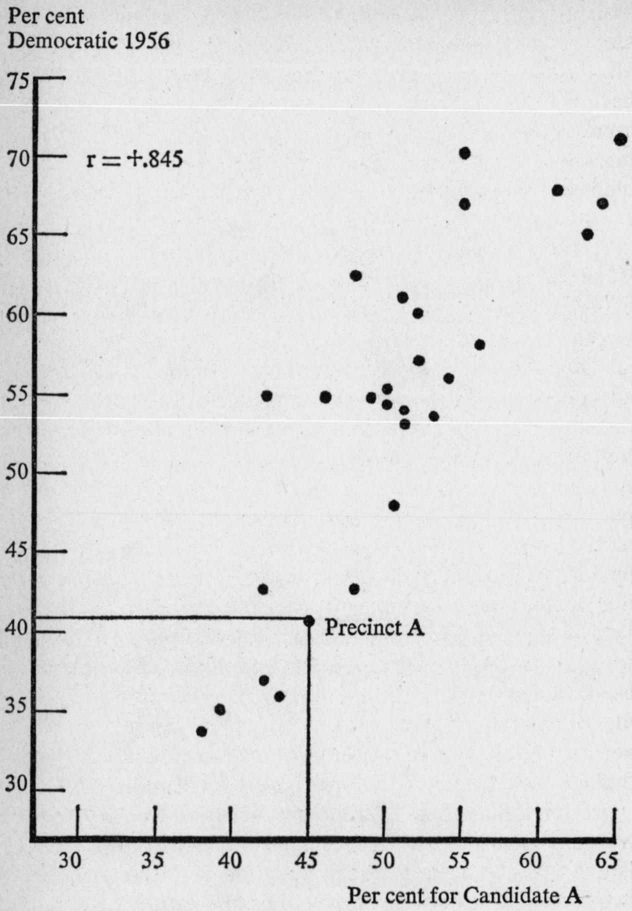

Per cent
Democratic 1956

75
70
65
60
55
50
45
40
35
30

r = +.845

Precinct A

30 35 40 45 50 55 60 65

Per cent for Candidate A

the range of perfectly positive to zero to perfectly negative. This measure is called the coefficient of correlation, usually identified as "r". Its meaning and a simple method of calculating it are lucidly explained in Key, *A Primer of*

Statistics, pp. 105-24. In this case, r = +.845, which is "fairly high." Just how significant the height of r is can also be given precise numerical meaning, that is, one can also calculate the likelihood that this figure could have been achieved by chance. Most textbooks of statistics have tables showing whether or not a given correlation including a given number of items could have been achieved by chance 1 per cent or 5 per cent of the time. In this case r = +.845 is within the .01 level of significance.)

It was then up to the student to interpret this result. What, if anything, did the correlation prove about his hypothesis that partisan considerations had influenced the voting? Strictly speaking, of course, it proved nothing at all about the motives of voters; one would have to take an opinion poll to begin to do that. What it did show was that there was a fairly strong tendency for those who had supported the Democrat for Congress to support Candidate A for judge. Considering the assertion of a number of people active in the election that the voters they knew were motivated by partisan considerations, this finding on behavior tended to support the hypothesis on motives. While this conclusion is superficially disputed by the fact that a known Democrat lost and a half-acknowledged Republican won in a generally Democratic county, the discrepancy can be explained by the facts that the outcome was close and that the correlation is not perfect. Clearly Candidate B was able to attract enough Democratic votes to win, even though most Democratic voters voted for Candidate A.

At this point it is appropriate, however, to insert the warning usually found in elementary discussions of correlation. Just because a high correlation is found between two variables, it does not follow that one causes the other. Students are often inclined to infer that, because a high correlation is found between, for example, average income and Republican voting, it follows that high income causes Republicanism. They both may be influenced by some third factor, to which a causal influence may properly be attributed. Thus, in the case here discussed, persons did not vote for Candidate A because they voted for the Democratic candidate for Congress in the previous election. Presumably they performed both actions because they were Democrats.

* * *

The foregoing example of simple statistical verification of a hypothesis about voting behavior is illustrative of one fairly obvious but fairly seldom performed statistical test of a political assertion. Appendix I-E, which contains a list of some writings in which various statistical tests have been applied to political data, will suggest other points at which you could perform your own tests of assertions gathered in the field. Further kinds of hypotheses often arrived at during field work that can be statistically tested, are:

1. When it is asserted that there is a long-term trend of voter affiliation from one party to another, you can establish the existence of a trend and, if it exists, how sharp it is, by the calculation of a time series trend (cf. Key, *A Primer of Statistics*, pp. 28-104). This is a particularly important kind of assertion to test, for often those who make it are thinking of but one or two elections, which are certainly not enough to establish a trend.

2. When it is asserted that a racial issue controls the voting in an area, it is possible to correlate the average number of votes by precincts or wards or counties for candidates with similar attitudes on racial issues with the number of whites (or colored) according to the most recent census or census estimates for the same districts.

3. When it is asserted that some sort of economic classification controls the voting habits of an area, it is often possible to correlate some sort of economic index for subdivisions of the area (such as assessed valuations for subdivisions which can be obtained from assessors' or treasurers' offices and which are usually kept by the same

civil divisions as those used in voting) with party votes in the same subdivisions.

4. Occasionally it is possible to make a multiple correlation of indices about several factors believed to influence voting behavior with voting by precincts or census tracts (for instance, party voting with assessed valuation, country of birth, and color). Often such mutiple correlations are sufficient to explain the voting of a neighborhood almost entirely (cf. Key, *op. cit.*, pp. 130-153).

5. When it is asserted that, for example, pro votes on a school bond issue are positively associated with new neighborhoods where there are many young children, this can often be checked by correlation of voting with school population or potential school population by precincts. School population data is often obtainable from school boards or superintendents of schools, sometime by civil districts, more often by school districts or square blocks. This is often an interesting assertion to test because it is often not provable.

APPENDIX I

Selected Bibliography on Local Politics

A. Analyses of Local Political Forces:

To borrow a word from the sociologists, this rubric might be called "political ecology." The most substantial and informative work in this area is undoubtedly V. O. Key, *Southern Politics in State and Nation* (New York, Knopf, 1949), a book which has here been suggested more than once as a model for student research. Two works which, although primarily reports on elaborate public opinion polls, nevertheless contain much sensitive detail on the politics of the communities surveyed, are:

Paul Lazarsfeld, Bernard Berelson, and Hazel Gaudet, *The People's Choice: How the Voter Makes Up His Mind in a Presidential Campaign*, 2nd edition (New York, Columbia University Press, 1948). Report of a survey of Erie County (Sandusky), Ohio, during the Roosevelt-Willkie campaign of 1940.

Bernard Berelson, Paul Lazarsfeld, and William McPhee, *Voting: A Study of Opinion Formation in a Presidential Campaign* (Chicago, University of Chicago Press, 1954). Report of a survey in Elmira, New York, during the Truman-Dewey campaign of 1948.

While many so-called community studies contain excellent detail on the political life of the community, one of these, which concerns a rural New York town, seems to me to have outstanding value for the political scientist: Arthur J. Vidich and Joseph Bensman, *Small Town in Mass Society: Class, Power, and Religion in a Rural Community* (Princeton, Princeton University Press, 1958), especially pp. 108-222.

B. Analyses of Local Political Forces (by Area):

While the books listed in Section A are, in my opinion, the best studies available to serve as models of student work, this bibliography is intended not only to provide models but also to list works that will help in understanding the political background of a particular community. Hence in this section I also list a number of works that in one way or another contain useful descriptions of local political scenes.

In 1952 a committee of the American Political Science Association conducted a study of the Presidential nominating process by arranging, among other things, for a political scientist in each of the states to describe the selection of delegates to the national conventions of each party. While the purpose of these descriptions was primarily to analyze the selection process, each author had necessarily to describe the background of local politics as well. While, as might be expected of the product of a committee, the chapters vary in quality, the state by state descriptions in the report can serve as useful background material on politics at the state level. In some instances, local politics in particular cities is also described. These descriptions of state politics appear in volumes II-V of Paul T. David, Malcolm Moos, and Ralph M. Goldman, editors, *Presidential Nominating Politics in 1952* (5 vols., Baltimore, Johns Hopkins University Press, 1954).

In the late 1940's appeared several journalistic works that purported to describe local politics all over the nation. These are possibly the last examples of the sensational muckraking exposé of local politics, a genre of journalism that first attracted national attention with Lincoln Steffens, *The Shame of the Cities* (1904). Nevertheless, the following three works, despite a sensationalism that distorts as much as it illuminates, do contain some material that may provide students with some historical background for their own studies:

John Gunther, *Inside USA* (revised edition, New York, Harper, 1951). A state-by-state survey of politics.

Robert S. Allen, editor, *Our Fair City* (New York, The Vanguard Press, 1947) contains chapters on Boston, New York, Philadelphia, Miami, Birmingham, Cleveland, Detroit, Chicago, Milwaukee, Memphis, St. Louis, Kansas City, Denver, Butte, Seattle, San Francisco, and Los Angeles, each chapter by a journalist employed in the city.

Robert S. Allen, editor, *The Sovereign State* (New York, The Vanguard Press, 1949) contains chapters on Massachusetts, New York, Pennsylvania, Georgia, Ohio, Illinois, Wisconsin, Louisiana, Nebraska, Texas, Utah, and California, each chapter by a journalist employed in the state.

Finally, although it is now quite out of date, Harold F. Gosnell, *Grass Roots Politics: National Voting Behavior of Typical States* (Washington, American Council on Public Affairs, 1942) contains analyses of political forces and tendencies in Pennsylvania, Wisconsin, Iowa, California, Illinois, and Louisiana and has, therefore, considerable value in providing an historical understanding of the politics of these states.

Arranged by areas of the country, here follows a list of reasonably adequate (or even, in some instances, superior but brief) descriptions of local politics:

The Northeast

Berelson, *et al., Voting* (see Section A). Elmira, New York.

Vidich and Bensman, *Small Town in Mass Society* (see Section A). Upstate New York.

Donovan, *Congressional Campaign* (see Section D). Lewiston, Maine.

William Foote Whyte, *Street Corner Society: The Social Structure of an Italian Slum* (2nd edition, enlarged, Chicago, University of Chicago Press, 1955, originally published 1943). This sociological study of especially the youth in an Italian section of Boston contains valuable though scattered descriptions of political habits, structures, and events.

W. Lloyd Warner and Paul S. Lunt, *Social Life in a Modern Community* (Volume I of the Yankee City Series, New Haven, Yale University Press, 1941). Although this anthropological survey of Newburyport, Massachusetts, is based on data now 25 years old—this was the first anthropological survey of a non-primitive American community—it nevertheless contains much political detail that is probably still valid and useful.

Warren Moscow, *Politics in the Empire State* (New York, Knopf, 1948). An exceptionally able journalist has here described the politics of New York State, with emphasis on the cleavage between New York City and the upstate area.

Earl Latham, *Massachusetts Politics* (New York, The Citizenship Clearing House, no date). This citizens' guide contains two excellent, though brief, chapters on the political background and political parties of Massachusetts.

Kelly, *Professional Public Relations* (see Section D). Maryland.

Fenton, *Politics in the Border States* (see this section, The Midwest). Maryland.

Granville Hicks, *Small Town* (New York, Macmillan, 1946). This somewhat sentimental and highly personal interpretation of a Connecticut village contains one short but interesting chapter on town politics (pp. 183-94).

Edward F. Cooke and G. Edward Janosik, *Guide to Pennsylvania Politics* (New York, Henry Holt, 1957). While this citizen's manual consists mostly of a description of the legal organization of parties, it does begin with a good brief outline of Pennsylvania political forces and party factions.

McKean, *The Boss* (see Section C). Jersey City, New Jersey.

Kurtzman, *Methods of Controlling Votes in Philadelphia* (see Section C).

The Midwest

Lazarsfeld, *et al., The People's Choice* (see Section A). Sandusky, Ohio.

John A. Kinneman and Shirley E. Shipley, "The Ecology of Pluralities in Presidential Elections," *American Sociological Review,* Vol. 10 (1945), pp. 382-89. This is an excellent and brief analysis by precincts of voting behavior and population characteristics in Bloomington, Illinois, and may well serve as a model for one kind of research that is possible for undergraduates.

Harder, *Non-Partisan Election* (see Section D). Wichita, Kansas.

W. Lloyd Warner, Wilfrid C. Bailey, *et al.*, *Democracy in Jonesville: A Study in Quality and Inequality* (New York, Harper, 1949). Presumably about a town in Northern Illinois, this sociological study contains an excellent analysis of party politics at pp. 214-36.

James West, *Plainville, U.S.A.* (New York, Columbia University Press, 1945). This sociological study of a small town in the southern midwest contains one excellent chapter on politics, pp. 85-91.

Leon Epstein, *Politics in Wisconsin* (Madison, University of Wisconsin Press, 1958). This is probably the best book available about the politics of a particular state. A number of the special studies in it may suggest studies that students can make about the other areas.

Fay Calkins, *The CIO and the Democratic Party* (Chicago, University of Chicago Press, 1952). This study contains analyses of the role of the CIO in 5 campaigns and incidentally therefore also contains interesting but rather sketchy descriptions of local politics from the point of view of a politically ambitious interest group. The five elections for which campaigns were analyzed are: The Ohio Senatorial campaign of 1950 (Taft-Ferguson); Steubenville, Ohio, congressional campaign of 1950 (Wayne Hays); the Democratic primary in the 5th Senatorial district of Illinois (Chicago) of 1950; the Democratic primary of 1950 for precinct captains in Winnebago County (Rockford), Illinois; and the Michigan general election of 1950.

John H. Fenton, *Politics in the Border States: A Study of the Patterns of Political Organization, and Political Change, Common to the Border States—Maryland,*

West Virginia, Kentucky, and Missouri (New Orleans, The Hauser Press, 1957). This work is an attempt to do for the border states what Key's *Southern Politics* did for the South. While it contains much useful material especially in its case studies of county politics, it is less impressive than its model.

P. Turano, *The Organization and Operation of the Democratic Party of Wayne County, Michigan* (Ann Arbor, Michigan, Edwards Brothers, 1953) contains useful background material on Detroit politics.

Joseph G. LaPalombara, *A Guide to Michigan Politics* (New York, Citizenship Clearing House, New York University, 1955).

Alfred deGrazia, "The Limits of External Leadership over a Minority Electorate" (see Section D). Chicago.

Smith and Sarasohn, "Hate Propaganda in Detroit" (see Section D).

Martin Meyerson and Edward C. Banfield, *Political Planning and the Public Interest* (Glencoe, Illinois, The Free Press, 1955). As a study of the administration of housing in Chicago, this work incidentally contains an excellent picture of some facets of Chicago politics.

Gosnell, *Machine Politics: Chicago Model* (see Section C).

Milligan, *Missouri Waltz* (see Section C).

Clarence A. Berdahl, Robert S. Friedman, Robert E. Scott, and W. Carl Wimberly, *Democratic Presidential Politics in Illinois, 1952: Report on the Illinois Delegation to the Democratic National Convention* (Urbana, Institute of Government and Public Affairs, University of Illinois, 1954). As an outgrowth of David, *et al., Presidential Politics in 1952,* this work contains some detail on Democratic party organization and factions.

The South

Key, *Southern Politics* (see Section A).

John Dollard, *Caste and Class in a Southern Town* (New York, Harper, 1957). While the material on politics is somewhat scattered through the book, still it is an excellent sociological study of a Southern black belt community and for this reason is also of great importance for the study of local politics in small southern towns. See especially chapter 10.

Allison Davis, Burleigh B. Gardner, and Mary R. Gardner, *Deep South: A Social Anthropological Study of Caste and Class* (Chicago, University of Chicago Press, 1941). While this study is as a whole less impressive than Dollard's, its comments on politics are more systematic and are collected in one chapter, pp. 483-538.

Leonard Reissman, K. H. Silvert, and Clifford W. Wing, "The New Orleans Voter: A Handbook of Political Description," *Tulane Studies in Political Science,* Vol. II (1955).

Kenneth N. Vines, "Republicanism in New Orleans," *Tulane Studies in Political Science,* Vol. II (1955).

Floyd Hunter, *Community Power Structure: A Study of Decision Makers* (Chapel Hill, University of North Carolina Press, 1953). This sociological study of leadership in a large industrial city of the southeast contains a good brief description of the city's politics, pp. 151-71.

Perry H. Howard, *Political Tendencies in Louisiana, 1812-1952* (Baton Rouge, Louisiana State University Press, 1957) contains a lengthy chapter on the 1952 election and beyond and may be said to supersede an earlier article on this subject: Rudolph Heberle and Perry H. Howard, "An Ecological Analysis of Political Tendencies in Louisiana in the Presidential Election of 1952," *Social Forces,* Vol. 32 (1954).

Ogburn and Grigg, "Factors Related to the Virginia Vote on Segregation" (see Section E).

Hugh D. Price, *The Negro and Southern Politics: A Chapter of Florida History* (New York, New York University Press, 1957). This volume supersedes the author's essay "The Negro and Florida Politics, 1944-54," *Journal of Politics,* Vol. 17 (1955).

Weeks, *Texas One-Party Politics in 1956* (see Section D).

O. Douglas Weeks, *Texas Presidential Politics in 1952* (Austin, Institute of Public Affairs, University of Texas, 1953). This and the following study are outgrowths of work undertaken for David, *et al., Presidential Nominating Politics in 1952,* and are both more detailed and more successful than most of the state chapters in that work.

L. Vaughn Howard and David R. Deener, "Presidential Politics in Louisiana, 1952," *Tulane Studies in Political Science,* Vol. 1 (1954).

William Goodman, *Inherited Domain: Political Parties in Tennessee* (Knoxville, Bureau of Public Administration, University of Tennessee, 1954).

Doherty, "Liberal and Conservative Voting Patterns in Florida" (see Section E).

Robert T. Daland, *Dixie City: Portrait of Political Leadership* (Bureau of Public Administration, University of Alabama, 1956).

Reynolds, *Machine Politics in New Orleans* (see Section C).

The West

Dean R. Cresap, *Party Politics in the Golden State* (Los Angeles, The Haynes Foundation, 1954). Although this is primarily a study of organization, it contains much material on political trends and leadership.

M. R. Merrill, ed., "The 1954 Elections in Eleven

Western States," *Western Political Quarterly*, Vol. 7 (1955), pp. 589-635, consists of brief but informative articles on the politics of Arizona, California, Colorado, Idaho, Montana, Nevada, New Mexico, Oregon, Utah, Washington, and Wyoming.

Joseph P. Harris, *California Politics* (Stanford, Stanford University Press, 1955) contains an excellent, though brief, analysis of party factionalism.

Hugh A. Bone, *Grass Roots Party Leadership: A Case Study of King County, Washington* (Seattle, Bureau of Government Research, University of Washington, 1952). This is an analysis of the Republican precinct leaders in Seattle.

Kelly, *Professional Public Relations* (see Section D) contains a study of the firm of Whitaker and Baxter and its role in California politics.

C. Descriptions of the Old-fashioned Political Machines: One of the earliest interests of professional political scientists was the urban political machine. While many of their descriptions of such machines are colored by an excessive emotional zeal for bringing an end to corruption, some of these books have become classic studies of local politics. Since the old-fashioned machines have for the most part disappeared, these books are hardly relevant today; but I list some of the best of them (emotionally detached and empirically oriented ones) for they do give excellent historical background on urban politics. In several instances, also, remnants of the machines are still in existence.

Harold F. Gosnell, *Machine Politics: Chicago Model* (Chicago, University of Chicago Press, 1937).

David H. Kurtzman, *Methods of Controlling Votes in Philadelphia* (Philadelphia, University of Pennsylvania, 1935).

Dayton D. McKean, *The Boss: The Hague Machine*

in Action (Boston, Houghton, Mifflin, 1940). Jersey City, New Jersey.

George M. Reynolds, *Machine Politics in New Orleans 1897-1926* (New York, Columbia University Press, 1936).

Maurice Milligan, *Missouri Waltz* (New York, Charles Scribner's Sons, 1948). Kansas City, Missouri.

D. Descriptions of Campaigns:

While not much descriptive material on local election campaigns has been gathered by social scientists, studies of campaigns are, as noted in the text, ideal for student analyses of politics, especially if the student is fortunate enough to obtain a suitable post for observation. Fortunately the few campaign studies that do exist are excellent models for student work. Recently the Eagleton Foundation at Rutgers University has undertaken to publish case studies in practical politics. The first two of these are reports on campaigns and can serve as a model for similar studies by students.

John C. Donovan, *Congressional Campaign: Maine Elects a Democrat* (New York, Henry Holt and Co. for the Eagleton Foundation, 1958). Although quite brief, this essay successfully combines observations on political structure and social forces with a detailed description of personalities and events in the 2nd Congressional district (Lewiston).

Marvin A. Harder, *Non-Partisan Election: A Political Illusion?* (New York, Henry Holt and Co. for the Eagleton Foundation, 1958). More personal and more concentrated on the details of events in Wichita, Kansas, than is Donovan's case study, this still manages to give an adequate picture of a local campaign. Furthermore, it is about the kind of campaign that students may often have an opportunity to observe closely.

Five studies in which excellent pictures of campaigns are incidental to their analyses of particular sorts of political behavior are:

Stanley Kelly, Jr., *Professional Public Relations and Political Power* (Baltimore, Johns Hopkins University Press, 1956). While this work is an analytic study of public relations men in politics, it contains an excellent case study of the Butler-Tydings Senatorial campaign in Maryland in 1950.

Alfred deGrazia, "The Limits of External Leadership over a Minority Electorate," *Public Opinion Quarterly,* Vol. 20 (1956), pp. 113-28. As a thinly disguised study of the voting behavior of Negroes in the Chicago mayoralty campaign (Daley-Merriam) of 1955, this also provides a good picture of one aspect of the mayoralty campaign.

Carl O. Smith and Stephen B. Sarasohn, "Hate Propaganda in Detroit," *Public Opinion Quarterly,* Vol. 10 (1946), pp. 24-52. This is a detailed study of propaganda in the Detroit mayoralty campaign of 1945. Its value is somewhat lessened by the authors' concern for one of the losing candidates.

Calkins, *The CIO and the Democratic Party* (see Section B, the Midwest) contains analyses of the effect of the CIO in five campaigns.

O. Douglas Weeks, *Texas One-Party Politics in 1956* (Austin, Institute of Public Affairs, University of Texas, 1957) conveys an excellent picture of factional strife.

Other, possibly useful material on campaigns is contained in:

John C. Bollens, *Appointed Executive Local Government: The California Experience* (Los Angeles, Haynes Foundation, 1952). The case studies (pp. 64-87) of campaigns for city manager plans are too brief and sketchy to serve as a model for student work. I mention them here, however, because students often have an opportunity to study such campaigns and may, therefore, find the comparative material helpful.

Donald R. McNeil, *The Fight for Fluoridation* (New York, Oxford University Press, 1958). Although this work suffers from a highly journalistic presentation, it relates the details of several fluoridation campaigns, a type of campaign students often have an opportunity to observe. See especially the chapters on Stevens Point, Wisconsin, and Seattle, Washington.

Many studies of campaigns appear in histories and biographies. Usually these are too brief or too general to serve as a model for student work. But in the following works the student will find excellent descriptions of campaigns of other eras:

Thomas Beer, *Hanna* (New York, Knopf, 1929), contains as an appendix a private report to his employer by the author's father on his part in the Ohio Senatorial campaign of 1898. As such it is a remarkable contemporary and uninhibited account by a participant.

Richard Luthin, *The First Lincoln Campaign* (Cambridge, Mass., Harvard University Press, 1944).

Edmund A. Moore, *A Catholic Runs for President: The Campaign of 1928* (New York, Ronald Press, 1955).

Noble E. Cunningham, Jr., *The Jeffersonian Republicans: The Formation of Party Organization, 1789-1801* (Published for the Institute of American History and Culture by the University of North Carolina Press, Chapel Hill, 1957), contains excellent chapters on the campaigns of 1796 and 1800.

J. A. Neprash, *The Brookhart Campaigns in Iowa,*

1920–26 (New York, Columbia University Press, 1932).

E. Uses of Statistical Techniques to Describe Political Forces and Tendencies:

As noted in the text, election results and demographic data can often be analyzed with profit by statistical techniques. No effort was made in the text, however, to introduce students to the use of them, chiefly because an excellent introduction already exists:

V. O. Key, Jr., *A Primer of Statistics for Political Scientists* (New York, Crowell, 1954). This exceptionally lucid and elementary presentation of both the assumptions and computational techniques for frequency distributions, time series, and correlations is simple enough for a good student to master on his own and as an incident to political research. (It contains no proofs of theorems, only verbal and geometrical explanations of the sense of them. Hence the mathematical aspect of statistics is held to a minimum, leaving only the assumptions and the arithmetic for students to understand.)

While specialists in public-opinion polling are usually well trained in statistical techniques, students of political parties are often entirely literary in their orientation. Hence, many instructors are often unaware of the possibilities of isolating and describing political forces and tendencies by statistics. In order, therefore, to suggest the variety of kinds of hypotheses about local politics that can be tested by statistical operations on electoral and demographic data, I offer this list of what seem to me very worthwhile achievements in this field. I might add that I am convinced that political scientists have not adequately exploited statistical interpretation of election data, partly, I suspect, because for the last two decades most statistically trained political scientists have been attracted into public-opinion polling. Lately, however, some political scientists have become interested in the direct interpretation of election results by statistics, possibly because they have begun to realize that public-opinion polling techniques can answer questions only about motivation, not about behavior.

Stuart A. Rice, *Quantitative Methods in Politics* (New York, Knopf, 1928). This remains a classic in the field and has repeatedly inspired and suggested later research.

William F. Ogburn and Charles M. Grigg, "Factors Related to the Virginia Vote on Segregation," *Social Forces,* Vol. 34 (1956), pp. 301-8.

Samuel J. Eldersveld, "The Influence of Metropolitan Party Pluralities in Presidential Elections Since 1920," *American Political Science Review,* Vol. 43 (1949), pp. 1189-1206.

Leon Epstein, *Politics in Wisconsin* (Madison, University of Wisconsin Press, 1958). See also for an earlier version of some of the material in this book: Leon Epstein, "Size of Place and the Division of the Two-Party Vote in Wisconsin," *Western Political Quarterly,* Vol. 10 (1956), pp. 138-50.

Vladimir Cervin, "Some Correlates of Voting Behaviour in the 1952 Quebec Elections," *Canadian Journal of Economics and Political Science,* Vol. 21 (1955), pp. 370-3.

Ralph and Mildred Fletcher, "Consistency of Party Voting from 1896-1932," *Social Forces,* Vol. 16 (1936), pp. 281-5.

H. F. Doherty, Jr., "Liberal and Conservative Voting Patterns in Florida," *Journal of Politics,* Vol. 14 (1952), pp. 403-15.

W. F. Ogburn and Estelle Hill, "Income Classes and the Roosevelt Vote in 1932," *Political Science Quarterly,* Vol. 50 (1935), pp. 186-93.

R. H. Dangerfield and R. H. Flynn, "Voter Motivation in the 1936 Oklahoma Democratic Primary," *Southwestern Social Science Quarterly*, Vol. 17 (1936), pp. 97-105.

F. Studies of Local Politics Abroad:
The first major empirical work on local politics was André Siegfried, *Tableau Politique de la France de l'ouest sous la Troisième République* (Paris, A. Colin, 1913), a work that remains a classic in spite of its occasionally embarrassing mystique of geography. It had little immediate influence although perhaps derivative from it is Rudolph Heberle, "The Ecology of Political Parties: A Study of Elections in Rural Communities in Schleswig-Holstein, 1918-1932," *American Sociological Review*, Vol. 9 (1944), pp. 401-14. Since the second World War, however, there has been great interest in empirical political science in both France and England. In *Cahiers de la Fondation Nationale des Sciences Politiques*, a number of volumes are devoted to *sociologie électorale*. I list here the ones that seem most imaginative and most likely to suggest ideas on research subjects for Americans:

Vol. 1: Charles Moraze, *et al.*, *Études de Sociologie Électorale* (Paris, A. Colin, 1947), especially Pierre George, "Étude Preliminaire des Conditions Économique et Sociale de la Vie Politique dans une Commune de la Seine: Bourge-la-Reine," pp. 67-87.
Vol. 9: André Siegfried, *Geographie Électorale de l'Andèche sous la III*[e] *Republique* (Paris, A. Colin, 1949).
Vol. 60: François Goguel, editor, *Nouvelle Études de Sociologie Électorale* (Paris, A. Colin, 1954).
Vol. 71: Pierre Clement and Nelly Xydias, *Vienne sur le Rhône: La Ville et les Habitants, Situations et*

Attitudes, Sociologie d'une Cité Francais (Paris, A. Colin, 1955).

Vol. 82: Maurice Duverger, François Goguel, Jean Touchard, editors, *Les Élections du 2 Janvier 1956* (Paris, A. Colin, 1957), especially the monographs on campaigns in particular communities.

See also from France: Jean Pataut, *Sociologie Électorale de la Nièvre an XX Siècle, 1902-1951* (Paris, Cujas, 1955). An interesting work about Chile in the Siegfried-Goguel tradition is Ricardo Cruz-Cole, *Geografia Electorale de Chile* (Santiago, Chile, Pacifico, 1952). In England, as well as France, there have been a number of interesting studies. The best by far is Mark Benney, A. P. Gray, and R. H. Pear, *How People Vote: A Study of Electoral Behaviour in Greenwich* (New York, St. Martin's Press, 1956). Other occasionally useful ones from England are:

David E. Butler, *The British General Election of 1955* (New York, St. Martin's Press, 1955).

David E. Butler, *The British General Election of 1951* (London, Macmillan, 1952).

S. B. Chrimes, editor, *The General Election in Glasgow, February, 1950* (Glasgow, Jackson, Son and Co., 1950).

From Canada, Walter O. Filley, "Social Structure and Canadian Political Parties: The Quebec Case," *Western Political Quarterly*, Vol. 9 (1957), pp. 900-14. Finally, from Australia, an excellent analysis of a campaign: Henry Mayer and Joan Rydon, *The Gwydir By-Election, 1953: A Study in Political Conflict* (Canberra, Social Science Monograph #3, Australian National University, 1954).

APPENDIX II

Bibliography of Election Data

It has often been remarked that in the United States it is far easier to obtain data on baseball or horse racing than on elections. Cynics have suggested, therefore, that we care more about games and gambling than about democracy. Actually, however, this sad situation is less a function of indifference than it is an accidental by-product of our peculiar federalism. In our federal system, it is the states that are charged with running the major elections. Hence it is the states that must publish the election returns. As with everything we leave up to the states, performance is uneven. Some states publish comprehensive and well-organized data; others publish brief summaries of returns; some turn the publication over to private companies who in turn vary widely in performance; one state (Arkansas) publishes nothing at all either publicly or privately. A complete bibliography of what the states or their agent publishers offer in this field is contained in United States Bureau of the Census, "Election Data in State Documents," *State Documents,* #2, October, 1944. (Although now fourteen years old, this bibliography is still accurate, so far as I can ascertain, except that the New Mexico *Blue Book* and the *Report* of the Secretary of the Commonwealth of Virginia no longer contain election returns.)

The most easily accessible election returns, although probably not the most useful ones, are the returns for Presidential elections by counties. These are available in the following sources:

New York *World-Telegram: The World Almanac and Book of Facts* (annual) contains election returns for President by states and counties for the two previous Presidential elections. Returns for a particular November election are published by January of two calendar years later so that this source is available sooner than any other.

Richard M. Scammon, ed., *America Votes: A Handbook of American Election Statistics* (New York, The Macmillan Company for the Governmental Affairs Institute, 1956 and 1958). These first two volumes of a regular series contain not only the 1952 and 1956 Presidential election returns by counties but also the returns by counties for governors and senators from 1954 to 1956.

Bureau of the Census, *Vote Cast in Presidential and Congressional Elections, 1928-1944* (Washington, Government Printing Office, 1946) contains the votes cast for President, senators, and representatives by states and counties.

Edgar Eugene Robinson, *They Voted for Roosevelt: The Presidential Vote 1932-1944* (Stanford, Stanford University Press, 1947) includes the Presidential returns by counties for the elections indicated.

Edgar Eugene Robinson, *The Presidential Vote, 1896-1932* (Stanford, Stanford University Press, 1934) and its supplement, *The Presidential Vote, 1936* (Stanford, Stanford University Press, 1940) contain the Presidential vote by states and counties for the indicated years.

W. Dean Burnham, *Presidential Ballots, 1836-1892* (Baltimore, Johns Hopkins University Press, 1955) contains the Presidential returns by states and counties with due regard for changes in county boundaries.

Returns for Congressional elections (for senators by states and for representatives by districts) are contained in *The Congressional Directory,* which is usually published semi-annually.

Returns for President, governor, and other state officials are collected in publications dealing with regions or states:

Alexander Heard and Donald S. Strong, *Southern Primaries and Elections, 1920-1949* (University, Alabama, University of Alabama Press, 1950) contains the election returns by counties in gubernatorial and senatorial elections for the period indicated as well as data by counties on some important referenda both in this period and earlier.

James R. Donoghue, *How Wisconsin Voted 1848-1954* (Madison, Bureau of Government, University Extension Division, University of Wisconsin, 1956) contains the returns by counties for Presidential, gubernatorial, and senatorial elections for the period indicated.

Jasper B. Shannon and Ruth McQuown, *Presidential Politics in Kentucky, 1824-1948* (Lexington, Bureau of Government Research, University of Kentucky, 1950) contains the Presidential vote by counties for the period indicated.

H. L. Alderfer and Fanette H. Luhrs, *Gubernatorial Elections in Pennsylvania, 1922-1946* (State College, Pennsylvania, Pennsylvania Municipal Publications

Service, 1946) contains gubernatorial votes by counties for the period indicated.

All the foregoing materials contain the vote by counties, which for most student purposes is quite inadequate since students need the election returns of those smaller civil districts which they can more easily study. Some of the states as well as New York City publish election data that is very good for this purpose, with the vote broken down by towns or wards or precincts as well as by counties. The publications in which the data appears, as well as a brief indication of its quality, are contained in the following list:

Connecticut: Secretary of State, *Connecticut Register and Manual* (annual). General election returns by counties and towns for national officials and state executive officials, and by districts and towns for state legislators.*

Illinois: Secretary of State, *Illinois Blue Book* (annual). Primary and general election returns by counties downstate and, in Cook county, by Chicago wards and townships outside of Chicago, for national officials and state executive officials; general election returns by districts for state judicial and legislative officials.

Iowa: Superintendent of Printing, *Official Register* (biennial). Primary returns by counties; general election returns by counties, cities, and precincts for national officials and state executive officials.

Maine: Fred L. Tower Companies, *Maine Register State Year-Book and Legislative Manual* (annual). General election returns by counties and towns for national officials and governor.

* "National officials" refers to President, senators and representatives in Congress; "state executive officials" refers to elected executives (governors, state treasurers, regents of state universities, etc.); "state judicial officials" refers to judges and in some states to prosecutors.

Massachusetts: Clerk of the Senate and Clerk of the House, *A Manual for the Use of the General Court* (biennial). General election returns by counties and towns for national officials and governor and by towns or districts for state legislators. (N.B. Boston returns are *not* broken down.)

Minnesota: Secretary of State, *Legislative Manual Compiled for the Minnesota Legislature* (biennial). Primary returns by counties, general election returns by counties, cities, and precincts for national officials and state executive officials; primary and general election returns by districts for state legislators.

Missouri: Secretary of State, *Official Manual* (biennial). Primary returns by counties, general election returns by counties, towns, wards, and precincts for national officials and state executive officials; primary and general election returns by districts for state legislators.

New Hampshire: Secretary of State, *Manual for the General Court* (biennial). This contains by far the best data of that published for any state. Primary and general election returns by counties, towns, and wards for all national, state executive, state legislative, and state judicial officials; primary and general election returns by counties for all elective county officials.

New Jersey: Publisher to the Legislature, *Manual for the Legislature of New Jersey* (annual). General election returns by counties, cities, and wards for national officials, governor, and selected county officials.

New York State: Secretary of State, *Manual for the Use of the Legislature of State of New York* (annual). General election returns by cities and counties for President, by counties for United States senator and state executive officials other than governor and lieutenant governor, by districts for state legislative and judicial officers and United States representatives, by counties, cities, and wards upstate and by counties and assembly districts in New York City for governor and lieutenant governor.

New York City: Commissioners of Elections, *Annual Report of the Board of Elections in the City of New York* (annual). General election returns by county and assembly district for mayor, borough president, council president, members of the council; state representatives, state senators, and state and municipal judges.

Ohio: Secretary of State, *Ohio Election Statistics* (biennial). Primary and general election returns by county for national and state executive officials, members of political party state committees and county officials; primary and general election returns by districts for national and state legislative officials.

Pennsylvania: Department of Property and Supplies, Bureau of Publications, *The Pennsylvania Manual* (biennial). Primary returns by counties for national officials and state executive officials; general election returns by counties, cities, wards, and precincts for President, by counties for state executive officials and United States senators, by district for representatives in Congress and state legislators.

Rhode Island: Secretary of State, *Manual with Rules and Orders for the Use of the General Assembly of the State of Rhode Island* (biennial). General election returns by counties and cities for President, by cities, wards, and precincts for governor, by districts for representatives in Congress.

Wisconsin: Legislative Reference Library, *The Wisconsin Blue Book* (biennial). Primary and general election returns by counties, cities, and wards for national officials and state executive officials. Primary returns by parties and by counties, cities, and wards for delegates to national conventions.

Wyoming: Secretary of State, *Official Directory and Election Returns* (biennial). General election returns

APPENDIX III

Other Sources of Statistical Data

For an essay on the voting habits of a community, of the sort described in Chapter II, and for statistical verification of assertions by informants in the manner suggested in Chapter IX, you need to gather numerical data about the community. This appendix is intended to suggest several sources for it.

Election Returns:
As pointed out in Chapter IV and in Appendix II, state legislative manuals sometimes contain recent state and national election returns by wards and even by precincts. The detailed returns of local elections and the local detail of state and national elections are available from city, town, or county clerks (or registrars). Clerks also have

registration data for the community they serve. State law usually obligates clerks and registrars to show election and registration data to any citizen who asks for them.

Census Statistics:

For all those who write about a neighborhood in any one of the metropolitan areas listed in Table I, selected population and housing characteristics are available for areas called "census tracts." Census tracts are "small areas, having a population usually between 3,000 and 6,000, into which certain large cities (and sometimes their adjacent areas) have been subdivided for statistical and local administrative purposes." They are approximately uniform in population; they are constructed with "due regard for natural features"; and they are "designed to include an area fairly homogenous in population characteristics." "In cities where the ward lines are infrequently changed, the tracts may form subdivisions of the wards; but they are usually laid out without regard to the ward boundaries."

The purpose of these statistics is, of course, to provide population data for areas smaller than town or counties, in order to permit "the study of neighborhoods."

TABLE I

List of Cities Subdivided into "census tracts" by the Bureau of the Census

1. Akron, Ohio*
2. Atlanta, Georgia*
   Atlantic City, New Jersey
   Augusta, Georgia*
3. Austin, Texas
4. Baltimore, Maryland*
5. Birmingham, Alabama
6. Boston, Massachusetts*
7. Bridgeport, Connecticut*
8. Buffalo, New York*
9. Chattanooga, Tennessee*
10. Chicago, Illinois*
11. Cincinnati, Ohio*
12. Cleveland, Ohio*
13. Columbus, Ohio*
14. Dallas, Texas*
15. Dayton, Ohio*
16. Denver, Colorado*
    Des Moines, Iowa*
17. Detroit, Michigan*
18. Duluth, Minnesota
19. Durham, North Carolina*
    Elizabeth, New Jersey
20. Flint, Michigan*

21. Fort Worth, Texas*
22. Greensboro, North Carolina*
23. Hartford, Connecticut*
24. Houston, Texas*
25. Indianapolis, Indiana*
    Jersey City, New Jersey*
26. Kalamazoo, Michigan*
27. Kansas City, Missouri*
28. Los Angeles, California*
29. Louisville, Kentucky
    Macon, Georgia*
30. Memphis, Tennessee
31. Miami, Florida*
32. Milwaukee, Wisconsin*
33. Minneapolis-St. Paul, Minnesota*
34. Nashville, Tennessee*
    Newark, New Jersey
35. New Haven, Connecticut
36. New Orleans, Louisiana
37. New York, New York
38. Norfolk, Virginia*
39. Oklahoma City, Oklahoma*
40. Omaha, Nebraska
41. Paterson, New Jersey*
42. Philadelphia, Pennsylvania*
43. Pittsburgh, Pennsylvania*
44. Providence, Rhode Island*
45. Richmond, Virginia
46. Rochester, New York
47. St. Louis, Missouri*
48. San Diego, California*
49. San Francisco-Oakland, California*
50. San Jose, California*
    Savannah, Georgia*
51. Seattle, Washington*
52. Spokane, Washington
53. Springfield, Massachusetts*
54. Syracuse, New York*
55. Tacoma, Washington*
56. Toledo, Ohio
57. Trenton, New Jersey
58. Utica, New York*
59. Washington, District of Columbia*
60. Westchester County, New York
61. Wichita, Kansas
62. Honolulu, Hawaii*

* Indicates that the adjacent metropolitan area is divided into census tracts.

Note: Cities without numbers are divided into tracts, but no statistics were issued for them for the 1950 census.

Since your research is the study of a neighborhood, census tract statistics are ideal for your purpose. The data on population for each census tract includes numbers of people by sex, age, race, country of birth, and marital status (with or without households). The socio-economic data for each census tract includes numbers of families and unrelated individuals, numbers of households, numbers of families and unrelated individuals classified by income groups, numbers of adults classified by grade of school completed, numbers of persons in various employment statuses (self-employed, unemployed, etc.), numbers of persons in various occupation groups (professional workers, laborers, etc.), etc. The data on housing, which is a kind of socio-economic index, classifies dwellings for each census tract by kind of tenancy (owner or renter occupied), by the number of dwelling units in one building, by the condition of the plumbing, by the year built, by the number of persons per dwelling unit, by the number of persons per room, by the kind of heating and refrigeration, by the possession of television, and by rent or value of the dwelling. All of this data may on occasion be politically relevant, especially in comparison with other tracts in the same city which have a different political complexion.

For census tract data, see: U.S. Bureau of the Census, *U.S. Census of Population: 1950,* Vol. III, *Census Tract Statistics* (in 62 parts, all of which have been published in separate bulletins), U.S. Government Printing Office, Washington 25, D.C., 1952.

For those not fortunate enough to study an area divided into census tracts, similar data may be gathered from the following sources:

U.S. Bureau of the Census, *U.S. Census of Population: 1950,* Vol. II, *Characteristics of the Population* (in 54 parts), U.S. Government Printing Office, Washington 25, D.C., 1952.

U.S. Bureau of the Census, *U.S. Census of Housing,* Vol. I, *General Characteristics,* Vol. II, *Non-Farm Housing,* U.S. Government Printing Office, Washington 25, D.C., 1953.

These three volumes contain more extensive data of the kind contained in the census tract series. Unfortunately for your purposes, it is not as conveniently arranged and it is broken down into less usable units. These volumes present the data for urban places of 10,000 or more population, for urban places or urbanized areas of 2,500 to 10,000, and for counties. They also present less detailed data for urban places of 1,000 to 2,500.

Special population studies which may occasionally be useful are:

U.S. Bureau of the Census, *U.S. Census of Population: 1950,* Vol. IV, *Special Reports,* U.S. Government Printing Office, Washington 25, D.C., 1954.

1. Part 3, Chapter A, *Nativity and Parentage.* This bulletin is especially valuable for determining the economic status of foreign born whites in the 162 standard metropolitan areas.
2. Part 3, Chapter B, *Non-White Population by Race.* This bulletin is valuable for areas in which a substantial number of Orientals and Indians live.
3. Part 3, Chapter C, *Persons of Spanish Surname.* This bulletin is useful for determining the economic characteristics of the Spanish population of the Southwest.
4. Part 3, Chapter D, *Puerto Ricans in Continental United States.* This bulletin is, of course, chiefly useful for New York City.

Economic Statistics:

Bureau of the Census reports are also very useful in describing the economic characteristics of the area you study. For urban areas, statistics about the kind of industry, the variety of occupations, classifications, and medians of income, etc. are conveniently set forth in:

U.S. Bureau of the Census, *County and City Data Book, 1952* (*A Statistical Abstract Supplement*), U.S. Government Printing Office, Washington 25, D.C., 1953.

The *County and City Data Book* is an exceptionally useful study; but, unfortunately, it does not offer data for units smaller than cities or counties.

Reports on the numbers of persons covered by Social Security, arranged by occupation and by the size of the employing firms, are given for each county in:

U.S. Bureau of the Census and U.S. Bureau of Old Age and Survivors' Insurance, a cooperative report, *County Business Patterns, First Quarter, 1953,* in 10 parts, U.S. Government Printing Office, Washington 25, D.C., 1954.

For information about the economy of rural areas, the U.S. Census of Agriculture is invaluable. The smallest unit for which data is given in this census is the county; but this is not in this instance a serious handicap for the purposes of political studies:

U.S. Bureau of the Census, *U.S. Census of Agriculture, 1950,* Vol. I, *Countries and State Economic Areas* (in 34 parts), U.S. Government Printing Office, Washington 25, D.C., 1952-53.

It includes data by counties on the acreage, value, size, and facilities and equipment of farms; on the number of farm operators; on the tenure of operators; on the quantity of livestock; and on the quantity of crops harvested.

One special report of the Census of Agriculture is especially valuable for studies in the West, where irrigation and water are often intensely burning public issues:

U.S. Bureau of the Census, *U.S. Census of Agriculture, 1950,* Vol. III, *Irrigation of Agricultural Lands,* U.S. Government Printing Office, Washington 25, D.C., 1953.

Privately Collected Statistics:

In addition to the Bureau of the Census, some private research firms study buying areas in terms of income, expenditures, etc., following for the most part the categories established by the Census Bureau. These studies are usually paid for by a local trade association (the chamber of commerce, for example), from whom you can in most instances get the report. If they have been carefully collected, these data are valuable, especially since they are likely to be more recent than the census.

Labor-union membership data, which are often politically relevant, can sometimes be obtained from the local Trades and Labor Council (AFL) and the local Industrial Union Council (CIO), which organizations are the central bodies in each city to which most local unions belong. Such statistics are often overstated, however, especially when they are given verbally. If one union is particularly influential in your locality (as, for example, the United Rubber Workers is in Akron, Ohio), then it is probably worthwhile to consult the most recent report of the national convention of that union. (If the union is important locally, very possibly the public library has a copy of the convention report. Most large university libraries collect union convention reports. And, of course, local business agents are very likely to have a copy that they can lend you.) With the convention report, you can roughly estimate the membership of local unions in your community on the basis of their representation in the national convention.

Church membership statistics are also occasionally relevant to politics. But they are difficult to obtain. The Census Bureau has not studied church affiliation since 1936; hence its count is so far out of date as to be useless. Occasionally local Councils of Churches conduct a religious census (usually with a view toward establishing new churches in new neighborhoods); and, if such a census is recent and accurate, it is, of course, valuable. Several archdioceses of the Roman Catholic Church have recently conducted a careful and accurate census of Catholics. Where available, it is, of course, highly valuable. Most religious leaders can estimate the relative membership of the several denominations in the community; but, in the absence of statistical verification, such estimates are likely to be distorted by bias and misinformation.

Maps:

Local politics cannot be studied without a thorough knowledge of local political divisions. Very few people, even old residents, know the exact boundaries of wards, precincts, etc. Hence, in order to learn the area and extent of the political subdivisions you study, you need a map. Furthermore, a map is an excellent addition to your finished essay.

For most cities and towns, private publishers print maps with ward lines on them. If such privately printed political maps are unobtainable, however, you can get the official descriptions of the political subdivisions in which you are interested from the city or county clerk (or the city or county surveyor); and with the official description, you can draw ward, precinct, township, etc., boundaries on any detailed map of the community.